Viral Verses

Art in Exceptional Times

Viral Verses

Art in Exceptional Times

**In aid of
NHS Charities Together Covid-19 Appeal**

Edited by Nicholas Linstead and Stephen Linstead

Acknowledgements

For support through our *GoFundMe* Appeal: Jo Brewis, Barbara Britton, Helen Brown, Michael Collier, Maggie Gothard, Jeanette Harrison, Sheila Hillier, Joan Hold, Susan Lutner, Kevin Jones, Jane Kelly, Carolyn Lewis, Graham Linstead, Garance Maréchal, Leo McCann, Margaret O'Grady, Cherisse Ofosu-Osei, Chris Pearson, Holly Randell-Moon, Pauline and Robin Grant, Rebecca Robinson, Charlotte Robson, Tony Rome, Dick Rosbiz, Jeep Siriviriyakul, Adam Swallow, Hugh Willmott, Yuli M. and six anonymous donors.

The Literary Consultancy

Gary Brannan of The Borthwick Press

Kim O'Sullivan of Design and Print Solutions, University of York

Helen Smith, Kate Pickett, Stuart Maconie, Aneta Horodecka-Kwiatek and John Leonard

Charitable Support Statement

100% of profits from this book will be donated to NHS Charities Together (registered charity no. 1186569). The estimated minimum donation per product sold is £3.00.

ISBN: 978-1-904497-69-1
First published 2020
Impression number 10 9 8 7 6 5 4 3 2 1

Copy edited by Stephen Linstead
Designed and typeset by Bryan Ledgard
Printed and bound by Design and Print Solutions, University of York
Published by The Borthwick Press, University of York

Dedication

This book is especially dedicated to the late
Edward Tudor 'Ted' Crum (23rd March 1947–4th April 2020)
a friend we lost to the Covid-19 virus.

It is also dedicated to the NHS workers and carers who
formed the front-line supporting those suffering from the virus,
and in the process lost their own lives;

And to the memory of all those young and old
who should still be with us but did not survive the
pandemic onslaught.

'Keep me in your heart for a while'
(Warren Zevon)

Contents

		page
Acknowledgements		**4**
Dedication		**5**
Contents		**7-9**
Foreword by Milly Johnson		**11**
Preface by Stephen Linstead		**12-13**
Introduction by Dame Margaret Drabble		**14-15**

Poet	Title	Illustrator	
Ian McMillan	*Two Old Men*	Graham Ibbeson	16-17
Stephen Linstead	*Curtains*	Aneta Horodecka-Kwiatek/	
		Mark K Allen	18-20
Mike Harding	*Tales from Tartary*	Jed Grimes	21-23
Mike Harding	*The Village*	Jed Grimes	24-25
Mike Harding	*This Little Place*	Jed Grimes	26-27
Monika Kostera	*Breathless, Again*	Tony Heald	28
Monika Kostera	*Elegies of the Living*		28-29
Chris The Poet Dibnah	*Family Rant*		30
Chris The Poet Dibnah	*Friendship*		31
Chris The Poet Dibnah	*Sharp, Bone-Handled Knife*	Bryan Ledgard	32-33
Chris The Poet Dibnah	*The Gates of Oz*		34
Roseanna Kettle	*The Return*	Helen Geddes	35
Roseanna Kettle	*Sollicitum*		36
Roseanna Kettle	*Relapse*		37
Roseanna Kettle	*Particles*		38
Roseanna Kettle	*Tableau Vivant*		39
Roseanna Kettle	*Data Ghost*		40
Roseanna Kettle	*Seedlings*		41
Roseanna Kettle	*Wreath*	Helen Geddes	42-43
Isabel Head	*Can You Hear Me?*	HTH	44
Isabel Head	*Pulling at Threads*	HTH	45
Anna Thornton	*Weaving*	Frances Sladen	46-47
Ray Hearne	*Prosecco/Enlightening/*	Robin Garside	48
	Four walls of Quarantine		49
Ray Hearne	*Thank You Please/Black Lives Matter*		50
Tia Duff	*Together*	Tia Duff	51
Jessie Summerhayes	*The Weeping*	Jessie Summerhayes	52-53
Jessie Summerhayes	*Islands Shout Shark*	Jessie Summerhayes	54-55
Jessie Summerhayes	*When Did We All Turn Green?*	Jessie Summerhayes	56-57
Jenny Knight	*Ode to Nigella*	Bryan Ledgard	58-59
Jenny Knight	*Breathing*	Mel Ledgard	60-61
Jenny Knight	*Virtual Purgatory*	Ian Meade	62-63
Jane Hilberry	*Before*		64

Lee Baskerville	*Technophobe*		65
Lee Baskerville	*Lockdown Breakdown*		66-67
David Weir	*Starling Dance*	Bryan Ledgard	68-69
David Weir	*Journeyman*		70
David Weir	*Bovine Social Spacing*	Bryan Ledgard	71
Natalie Saturnia	*Home*	Ian Meade	72-73
Natalie Saturnia	*Sunray*		74
Francesca Lea	*Turning Point*		75
John Law	*Thoughts in Isolation*	John Law	76-77
John Law	*Remember*		78-79
John Law	*Club*	Dave Howarth	80-81
John Law	*Summer Sunday*		82
Sophie Norton	*There is a Dangerous Man*		83
Sophie Norton	*Quarantine is a Circus*	Paul Gough	84-85
Cyang Stifano	*The Wind*	Stephen Cox	86
Chloe D'Arcy	*Drive-by lives*		87
Chloe D'Arcy	*Fishbowl*	Howard Aynhoe	88-89
Jenni Pascoe	*Encore/Gratitude/Metamorphosis*	Jed Grimes	90-91
Liz Deakin	*Plague Poems 1–6*	Liz Deakin	92-95
Maurice Rutherford	*Coronavirus*	Jeannie Clarke	96-97
Maurice Rutherford	*Lockdown Lunches*	Jeannie Clarke	98-99
Stephen Linstead	*Northern Exposure*	Aneta Horodecka-Kwiatek/ Mark K Allen	100-101
Stephen Linstead	*The Prospect Behind Us*	Barry Fox	102-103
Stephen Linstead	*Desert Meditation 1: Saguaro*	Aneta Horodecka-Kwiatek/ Mark K Allen	104-105
Eth Holmes	*Standing Tall*	Anne Genner Crawford	106-107
Eth Holmes	*Sweet Comfort*	John A McPake	108-109
Laura Potts	*Haiku sequence, Spring 2020*	Bryan Ledgard	110-111
Carina Riley	*We Are the Grandparents*	Stephen Cox	112-113
David Driver	*Shh, Don't Say a Word*	Bryan Ledgard	114-115
David Driver	*Four New Friends*		116
David Driver	*Lockdown*		117
Granville D Clarke	*John's Gone*	Granville D Clarke	118-120
Granville D Clarke	*Days and Trials of Fibrillation*		121
Sophie Ryall	*This Generation*		122-123
Sophie Ryall	*Trapped*	Anne Genner Crawford	124-125
Isabelle Lepore	*Ci Manchi Nonno*	wallpaperflare	126-127
Joe Solo	*She Is My Fighter Pilot*	Alan Andrews	128-129
Joe Solo	*This Is Our Blitz*	Alan Andrews	130-131
Amber Hawkins	*Listen For a Tweet*	Howard Aynhoe	132-133
Edsard Driessen	*Isolation*	Mel Ledgard	134-135
Rachel Feldberg	*Locked Down Pigeon*	Bryan Ledgard	136-137
Ellen Waters	*Bearing Fruit*	Charley Wright	138-139

Ellen Waters	Last Night	Charley Wright	140-141
Ellen Waters	Spring Cleaning	Paul Almond	142-143
Ellen Waters	Vow	Becky McMurray	144-145
Ellen Waters	Ghost Light	Becky McMurray	146-147
Aidan Quigley	Certificate		148
Aidan Quigley	Extenuating Circumstances		149
Aidan Quigley	Baptism	John A McPake	150-151
Brian W. Lavery	This Be the Monumental Verse …	Tony Heald	152-153
Brian W. Lavery	Times and Tides	Tony Heald	154-155
Rosemary Evans	Neighbourhood Watch	Bryan Ledgard	156-157
Adekunle Ridwan	Oh Land! (World Pandemic)	Mel Ledgard	158-159
Heath Common	Powis Square at 4am	Bryan Ledgard	160-161
Heath Common	When the Dog Bites the Monkey	Terry Brookes	162-163
Sophie Lutkin	Nightingale Street	Becky McMurray	164-166
Sophie Lutkin	Vulcan's Flame		167
Lynda Rose Morgan	Dad's Ladders	Bryan Ledgard	168
Rozana Ahmad Huq	Gratitude		169
Rozana Ahmad Huq	Born in Florence	Bryan Ledgard	170-171
Nes Vanriel-Edwards	The Seven Stages of Ignorant Grief		172
Louise Larkinson	Beached		173
Pamela Leadbetter	Shedding		174
Alice Manning	Scale		175
Alice Manning	Together But Apart	Mel Ledgard	176-177
Alice Manning	Viral/Virtual/Virus	Mel Ledgard	178-179
Gareth Griffith	Love in Lockdown	Terry Brookes	180-181
Matthew Walker	The Ruins at Babylon	Sophie Ioakim	182-183
Violet Hatch	91 Farm Road	Stephanie McRobert	184-185
Violet Hatch	Evenings in Isolation		186
Violet Hatch	The Visitor		187
Elizabeth Brown	Ode to Gerald	Bryan Ledgard	188-189
Hannah Ludlow	So Long		190
Hannah Ludlow	Disperse		191
Ralph McTell	Masks and Gowns	Ron Kiddier	192-193
Bev Bewley	Heligan	Marisha Bewley	194-195
Bev Bewley	Rings	Marisha Bewley	196-197
Stephen Linstead	Pandemic Low Tide in Holderness	Julie Gough	198-199
Ruth Roberts Owen	Cytokine Storm	Bryan Ledgard	200-201
Paul Thwaites	Silent Spring	Graham Ibbeson	202-203
Paul Thwaites	When I Thought You Were Gone	Graham Ibbeson	204-205
Paul Thwaites	High Numbers	Graham Ibbeson	206-207
Mel Ledgard	Charlottes and Garlands	Anne Genner Crawford	208-209
Paul Thwaites	NHS	Graham Ibbeson	210-211
Biographies			212-221
Contributors' Index			222

Foreword

Milly Johnson

We need poetry in our lives. It isn't a prerogative of the highbrow, it is for us all to enjoy. But people are afraid of poetry, worried they won't understand it, anxious that it will in some way exclude them. Yet, quite the opposite is true. Poetry connects writer with reader using a bridge of compact expression, richness of language and emotion made words. Poetry gives order to thoughts, captures feelings, displays them like fabulous artwork, gives us answers, or lets us find our own in its depths. Every word counts, every one has been chosen with care and positioned where it shines best; a beating heart visible in every piece. Here, in this anthology, it is a sharing of a world we are all locked into, trying to survive, trying to make sense of an unprecedented *now*. It is something to give us strength, awareness, comfort, optimism – not forgetting entertainment – through our precarious common experience.

This is a powerful and poignant collection of poems which has been spawned from this singular time. Beautiful words and illustrations from the perspectives of young and old minds, talents refined and raw, have been woven together into a stunning piece of art. There is sadness, despair, humour, hope within these glorious pages and, of course, a grand dollop of Yorkshire insight and wisdom. A truly magnificent coming together of creatives, and it makes me extra proud to read what my fellow 'God's own County' folk are capable of.

Milly Johnson
August 2020

Milly Johnson is an award-winning, Sunday Times best-selling British author of romantic fiction with over two million sales worldwide. She has written 18 full length novels and her book of cat-themed poetry, *A Cat-Shaped Space* (2019) raises money for Yorkshire Cat Rescue. She was winner of the Romantic Novelist's Association Award for Romantic Comedy in 2014 and 2016 and won their Outstanding Achievement Award in 2020. She is also an after-dinner speaker, poet, professional joke writer and newspaper columnist.

Photograph © Chris Sedgewick

Preface

In September 2019, I managed to reunite with an old University musician friend with whom I'd lost touch – Edward Tudor 'Ted' Crum. It was an emotional meeting but necessarily brief – I was doing a Roadshow in Coventry and he was preparing for a reunion of one of his former bands that coming Saturday in Warwick, when the Roadshow was playing in Brighton. Reflecting on the fact that we were too old to be doing this sort of stuff, we arranged to meet up again in the Spring. Sadly, it wasn't to be. Covid-19 took his life in early April.

It was agonising for his many friends not to be able to say goodbye to a much loved character. When I was younger I had learned a lot from him at a difficult time in my life. So I wrote a poem in his memory and shared it with Facebook friends. My eldest son, Nick shared it with some of his friends, and one of them offered to illustrate it. And so Nick's idea for this book was born. Bryan Ledgard offered to handle the design – the cover, internal layout, several of the illustrations, and general magic are his priceless contribution.

As the University of York was ground zero for UK Covid-19 cases, I asked colleagues whether they would be willing to support us and Prof. Kiran Trehan, Pro-Vice-Chancellor for Partnerships and Engagement was extremely helpful, arranging a pump-priming grant from the University's Partnership and Engagement Fund and support from the Vice-Chancellor, Professor Charlie Jeffery, to get us off the ground, and Gary Brannan arranged for the Borthwick Press to publish. Professor Helen Smith, Head of the Department of English and Related Literatures (and recent Internet sensation) promoted it to staff and students and many of them (including one sister and one mum) feature in the collection. We wanted York and Yorkshire to be the centre of gravity of the volume but in order to get it together quickly we depended on our existing networks and were therefore open to whatever came back from wherever we reached – so we have contributors from as far afield as Poland, Italy, Nigeria and Colorado, ranging in age from 16 to 98. The response was much greater than we anticipated and the present volume is around twice as big as our modest original plan.

Some of the poets are people whose work is well known. Ian McMillan is one of the country's best known and best loved poets. Mike Harding has been a celebrated performer, writer and broadcaster for half a century, although his fine poetry is less publicly familiar. Graham Ibbeson is perhaps the country's most popular sculptor, with over 40 public statues installed, but he also has an international reputation for his fine art work. Monika Kostera has published several books in two languages, and has even had her poems set to music on a jazz guitar album. Jeannie Clarke's familiar commissions include interior trompe l'oeil installations across the country and complex sets for the BBC. Yet the book also includes younger and part-time poets and illustrators, some publishing their work for the first time. We have poetic efforts by one or two people who would not describe themselves as poets but nevertheless are testimony to poetry's power as a personal medium.

The collection is aimed at the general reader, so our emphasis is on poetry that is accessible, but that does not exclude more demanding work that would sustain greater critical scrutiny. We invited poems that focused on directly viral experiences and reflections, people, observations and practices, but also those that resonated with moods and inflections that though unrelated may be evoked – from loss to joy, recollection to recovery, helpless isolation to passionate puissance, the future and the nature of memory, different ways of experiencing time, space and affect. We received a set of poems that really cover every inch of that terrain. Whilst we were not able to find an illustrator for each poem, and indeed some poems better suited standing unaided, we have been able to illustrate two-thirds of the poems and almost all the poets. Some poets chose to illustrate their own work.

So many of our friends have contributed their work and time and talent to this project and we are deeply grateful to them. They appear in the biographies at the end of the book. Others contributed to a *GoFundMe* project to ensure that we had the upfront liquidity needed to sign the necessary contracts and they deserve our warmest thanks.

But our greatest gratitude goes to the staff of the NHS and care homes who have borne so much risk in treating and caring for sufferers. The profits from this book will go to help those who continue to do so; the dedication of this book is to the memory of all those who lost their lives in trying to keep us all safe.

Hopefully this book will help us in dealing with often agonising memories, and will help to ensure that we continue to quietly celebrate their selfless sacrifice and keep alive the loving spirit in which it was made.

**Stephen Linstead
York
August 2020**

Photograph © Garance Maréchal

Dame Margaret Drabble is a novelist, critic and biographer who was born in Sheffield and educated at the Mount School, York, and Newnham College, Cambridge. An early member of the Royal Shakespeare Company in 1960, she soon established her reputation as a novelist with *A Summer Bird Cage* (1963) and *The Garrick Year* (1964). Her third novel, *The Millstone* (1965), won the John Llewellyn Rhys Memorial Prize in 1966, and *Jerusalem the Golden* won the James Tait Black Memorial Prize in 1967. In addition to 20 novels, she has published short fiction, full-length critical studies, articles, literary biographies, and edited two editions of *The Oxford Companion to English Literature* (1985, 2000). In 1991/92 she was a judge for the first Forward Poetry Prizes, widely considered to be poetry's equivalent of the MAN Booker Prize. In 2011, she was awarded the Golden PEN Award for 'a Lifetime's Distinguished Service to Literature'.

Photograph © Ruth Corney

Introduction

Dame Margaret Drabble

We turn to poetry in times of need. Poetry is with us at birth, at death, in sorrow and in celebration. We read it, we remember it, we recite it, and we write it. This volume is witness to the extraordinary power of poetry and the intensity of the times through which we have been living. Here is the concentrated history of the past few months. Poetry is what Wordsworth described as 'the spontaneous overflow of powerful feeling' – he claimed that it takes its origin from 'emotion recollected in tranquillity', and some of these poems do achieve a sense of calm, but many of them are instantly reactive and passionate. Reading through these very varied poems is a remarkable experience.

The poems cover a huge range of responses and poetic modes, from the tragic to the satiric and the comic, from the lyrical to the political and the enraged. We find free verse, sonnets, ballads, and haiku. Some react to the rapidly changing news of every day, with snapshots of contemporary events and their newly forged vocabulary, and others reach back to tragedies of the past, to the eruption of Etna and the story of the plague village of Eyam. There are poems from writers in their nineties, some describing particular responses to a unique and uniquely lonely situation, others stoically looking forward. There are poems from the young, enduring separation and stress, and poems about and for the care workers in the front line. Some celebrate a new and timeless sense of closeness to the natural world, with its starlings and pigeons and butterflies and symbolic nightingales, while others relay a sense of the indoor frustrations of lockdown. We journey between bird song and baked beans and Zoom. Some writers miss hugs, some are annoyed by other people complaining about missing hugs. Some of these poems make you laugh, and others bring tears to the eyes.

The main focus of the anthology is the coronavirus and the magnificent response to it made by the NHS. The virus appears in many forms, and has instantly become part of a whole new mythology, variously personified – an unseen monster, an ogre, an enemy. But we also find responses to the contemporaneous and entwined theme of Black Lives Matter, and several invoke the powerful image of the statue of the slave trader toppled into the dock at Bristol. We meet Philip Larkin's statue at the Paragon Station in Hull, which reminds us that this anthology originated in York, and many of its poems have a northern or specifically Yorkshire colouring. But it is also for all places, and for all of us who have been through these strange months together. Many voices and many ethnicities blend together here, in a fine and moving tribute both to the lost and to the survivors. If the NHS is our religion, poetry is a form of prayer.

Margaret Drabble
August 2020

Two Old Men in Caps in Barnsley, April 2020
Ian McMillan

Two old men in caps
Walk towards each other
In the April sun.
Years, they've known
Each other, years
Down the same pit.

One moves his head
To one side, ever so slightly
The other has begun
To do the same.
They move apart,
Two metres of pavement

Between them.
One says the other's
Name, one says
The other's name.
They walk on,
Socially distant

But part of each other.

Illustration: 'Graham' © Graham Ibbeson

Curtains (for Edward Tudor Crum)
Stephen Linstead

Through the crack in the curtains
I dimly, without attention,
Discern that a van is reversing
And we should steer clear.

Flickering, my mournful tablet
Shows a leathery hand – old, strong,
Fingers full of music
Touching a tiny one
With love and delicacy
Met by a curious fist
Clutching for wisdom.

It's a hand I once grasped and found full
Of friendship, fun, foolishness
Skill and streetwise laughter
And the will to keep a smile going
On our absurd mirthless journey.

We giggled our way through the white peak
On a cloud of herbs
In paroxysms at the silly sound
Of exotic words like paw-paw
On our urban English tongues.
We played and sang and danced
And clocked the devil's time sheet
With wistful wasteshifts that return unsquandered
In the memories that now repay me.

We took different roads but could hear each other
Just out of sight over the hill.
A crested hill, with sun on both sides
And joyful other company
Until the long descent brought our footsteps together
And we hugged. We'd never hugged before.
We'd never hug again.

He's gone to the plague that pushes us apart
Leaving only echoed happiness
And my curtains shut as though
My soul can't bear the sunshine.

continued overleaf …

Illustration © Aneta Horodecka-Kwiatek/Mark K Allen

Not today.

The van repeats its admonition
And I remember the same warnings
The night we had to evacuate when power cuts
Crashed the sewage farm next door
And the threat of a medieval epidemic
Secretly thrilled the history majors
While I delivered my thespian lines
In a bedsheet before boarding the bus.
That time comedy avoided tragedy
And we kept getting away with it
Until now.

Steer clear. Avoid. Stay alive.
Finally the van changes its trajectory and tune
And rumbles off.

And in this space of nothing but mindless birdsong
I can't summon the will
To open these curtains if I can't hold the world close
And laugh with it and hug with it and dance with it
Because somewhere in these things
The graphs and rates and ratios and algorithms
That divide and demean and render our humanity forfeit
Dissolve.

For now, words fail as breath expires
Meaning subsides to a hierophanic whisper
My old friend is needless and untimely gone
And our cliché lips freeze motionless paying the devil his due.
But, when we're safe,
Stay close, hear the echoes
Of the music he made
And the laughter he left
And make them ring again
So love is not lost and like the old religion
It bursts again into green shoots.
Remain unsplintered even when on different slopes
And share the redeeming sun that binds us all under one canopy.

He was my friend, and he is yours
When the curtains open up once more.

Tales From Tartary
Mike Harding

Now this didn't happen in my lifetime, or in your lifetime –
but it must have happened in somebody's lifetime
else how could I be telling you?
How an Irish seanchaí or storyteller would begin his tales.

What is there to tell? Too much.
Those sagas that the dancing days
Brought on the innocent breeze?
At first it was the gentlest touch:
Soft whisperings in the leaves;
A dog howl coming in the night
From some far farm huddled
Beneath the crags; the high,
Quiet rumour in the moonless sky
Of a travelling star that was
An airplane coming from the East –
Bringing no wise men bearing gifts.

That tapping on the windowpane,
Was it just wind-twitched twigs again,
Or praying, clutching, human bones?
Those voices? People? Or a neighbour's radio
Its practised, bloodless drone
Sowing curious gossip on the winter air?
Strange travellers' tales perhaps, half-heard,
Absurd, unravelling from Elsewhere?

But they were not your everyday myths
Of blemmyae, dragons, phoenix, manticores,
Of sciapods, mermen, basilisks or unicorns,
But something else come murderous subtle,
Served up quite invisible: a gas,
Miasmas on the wind, static in the air;
The pull of the full moon, perhaps,
That lifts the seas and folds them like soft cloth;
Some strange, molecular horseman coming near,
Riding westward at the speed of fear.

A man falls dead midstride, his soul departs
As he walks across a busy city square,

continued overleaf …

He lies and folk pass on by, the very air
Turns foul, a hug or grandchild's kiss
Can kill, and love itself mean death.
Lungs turn to glass, you bark for life,
Within hours the human castle falls,
Its engines locked solid with rust.
Small armies thread the air, invisible, dust;
It is there in everything you touch.

All comfort gone, nerves strung
Like winter branches on an angry sky. Some say
That we are living through
The close of Time, the End of Days,
God's displeasure, and they pray;
Others say it is our own bad dreams made flesh,
The tales we told ourselves of boogie men,
Of monsters from beyond the sun.

So many years we had been safe;
The bombs and gas, burning cities,
Famine, drought – the horsemen,
Without pity, remorseless riding out, the scythe
Held high, the banners flapping in the air –
But for so many years, always Elsewhere.

Now every little townland is Elsewhere,
And we discover that we have ourselves
Got strange fables and terrible tales to tell;
New brought from travellers in an antique land
They move amongst us and the tales are told,
As they sit by our fires, spinning their yarns;
New tales, hot tongued from Tartary,
Come with the caravans along the old Silk Road.

No magic carpet or Aladdin's lamp, or the tale
Of the Emperor's jewelled, automaton nightingale;
But the legend of that great market, and how
A host of rebel djinns emerged un-summoned
When the bottle was uncorked,
And how, unlike the huff and puff of the big, bad wolf,
Nobody noticed when the little piggies baulked,
Or saw the dust now wore the tyrant's crown,
As all our houses, big and small, came tumbling down.

Illustration © Jed Grimes

The Village
Mike Harding

Death in a bag of dandy clothes dances across
The high moorland, from London on a packhorse train.
The lead horse has a tree of bells, it sings out "Death is coming."
A song that no-one hears. How like a groom He comes;

And, one by one, by His kiss they are erased. Spirits leave,
And carcasses are heaped, "Bury your own"
They are told. The crows in the high trees
Dance and gibber to the long song of the spades

That ring below, pecking out graves
In the morning mist. Sun rises like a buboe,
And the sky turns black. They fear that God
Has left the world. Walking men drop,

As though the sky has struck them down. The people pray
To the moon, to the old gods, and some carve faces into trees.
Fever and flux, blood springs from every
Orifice, they post warnings and lock the world away.

A torque of silence rings the village, no one leaves
Or comes. On boundary stones the masons hack plague stoups,
Vinegar piscines where the sick leave coins
To pay for food and medicine from the world beyond.

And they waltz on with Death, turning their faces to the wall.
One woman buries eight – her husband and six children,
Yet lives. The old gravedigger too, is spared. After a year
They stare, blinking into the empty world, a shell.

The fire has died, the stoups are dried, crows mute,
Those who are left hear the returning pack horse bells
Ring out across a land half-mad,
That now no longer seems to know itself.

Illustration © Jed Grimes

This Little Place
Mike Harding

The sparrow that is a miracle
Pecks at the feeder as this most
Extraordinary everyday unfolds.
Air warmed by spring sun
Gives the daffodils a nudge,
A copper beetle glints and moves
Across the worn stone flags,
And a blackbird scolds and nags
Andrew the postie
Who walks on water on his rounds,
Whose hands are magically
Fitting letters through door slots,
Who has disturbed old Blackie at his task
Of tugging up the mystery that is a worm
From out the soil. Nothing we take
For granted any more, nothing is less
Than marvellous: that leaf, that bud
The blue and white bead of a jackdaw's eye;
That cat sliding along the wall eying the birds,
A puzzle of perfection in black fur;
That cloud capping the hill, those jackdaws
Cackling like black fireworks across the sky;
A day of miracles unfolds, each moment,
Telling itself stories in this teeming world.

Illustration © Jed Grimes

Breathless, Again
Monika Kostera

Flowers everywhere.
The spring began
with a checkmate.

Max von Sydow died.
A saint set out rambling –
she who died horribly
just for human companionship.
The year came undone.

No shoes, no regrets, elders leaving.
We drown in our heartblood
yet forgot
how to breathe.

This is not a mantra.
This is the broken way back
to the gardens.

Elegies of the Living
Monika Kostera

We did not fare so badly after all,
Not as poorly as
The things around us:

Cities, trees, hints, trivialities
We loved so much,

The kindness of strange places.
The blessed hormones

And the songs, the songs,
All the elegies of the living.

We did not fare as badly as so many things
That mattered, the giant shoulders,
We still keep handsome, where we stand.

We can do no other.

Illustration © Tony Heald

Family Rant
Chris the Poet Dibnah

This starts here
With the pen in the kitchen
At a stroke, with a smoke
Am I that poetry bloke?
Am I so lazy as sin
That I can't fit the time in
To offer words up to you
And try to do what I'm supposed to do
Best?
Pen a rhyme for the family
With a fire in my heart
Because you all mean so much to me….
Did you get lost in the fog
Had no trailer, no dog
Trying to find what you'd had
But on a bench feeling mad
With all the sites and the good times
Running on in your mind
All the festys and convoys
And all the people that shined?
And did you rise from the ashes
And know you were strong
Were you one in a million
And barmy and wrong?
Did I know you in the autumn
When the leaves obscured the track?
Did I see you in the winter?
Did you get your tenner back?
Sure I saw you in the springtime
When old trees feel shoots grow new
And I will see you in the summertime
And raise a glass to you,
I will see you when we party
With our mad, beloved crew.
I will bask in your forgiveness
Cos at times I've been a prat
But a prat of love, retiring
Getting homely wry and fat.

Friendship
Chris the Poet Dibnah

Precious and perfect
And gone with the dawn
Are the memories I keep
Of the friends that I mourn.
Rash and excited
and noisy and mad
Are the echoes I hear
Of the friends that I had.
Faces no more to be dirty and free
In the ditch of delirium looking at me
Teachers and welders
And parents of chavs
Are my family of wrongness
The friends that I have.

Sharp, Bone-Handled Knife
Chris the Poet Dibnah

It only takes five minutes
From a smart West London flat
Only takes five minutes
To a thin blade in the back
That's what the woman told him
'Twas the gist of what she'd said
He wanted proof she offered truth
And now he's lying dead.

He never knew that Death had stalked him
That she'd been there all the time.
When he visited the gypsy
She'd been three steps behind
And as his spirit left his body
He looked down but did not know
Who the strange girl was
With blade in hand
Not twenty feet below.

Never knew that out of boredom
And the urge to take a life
That Death herself had aimed the blow
With her sharp bone-handled knife.

Death is sitting waiting on the outskirts of L.A.
For a train that's packed with people
Which is heading out this way
You'll never know she's coming
When she does she never stays
But she's here right now
On the main branch line
On the outskirts of L.A.

Death is floating, dreaming
Five miles out from Tiger Bay
A ferry full of passengers
Is heading home today
And as the engine blew
The hull right through

Just one man knelt to pray
In the pouring rain
Of a howling gale
Just out from Tiger Bay.

Death is sitting smoking
On the slopes above Pompeii
Waiting on an old volcano
One which rarely likes to play
And the people down below her
Cannot know that it's today
That the ash will fall
Their lives will stall
And she will have her way.

If Soma, with its sweet allure
Were ever there to grace
the minds of men, you can be sure,
'Twas cut & bagged and sold as pure.
I made inquiries, most discreet
Was guided through back streets unto a door
With urgent need I thought of nothing more
Than this purchase, which I knew I must complete.
So I knocked, as I have on many doors
And wondered if I would on many more
As darkness fell I waited in the street
I hung on every sound with bated breath
'Twas then I heard the step of sandalled feet
No stranger at the door, but only Death.

She said –
There's one at the door
At the gate to salvation
There'll be room for one more
'Til the end of creation
There's one at the door
At the gate to damnation
There'll be room for one more
'Til the end of creation
There's one at the door.

Illustration © Bryan Ledgard

The Gates of Oz
Chris the Poet Dibnah

Here we are at the gates,
Of the great and powerful Oz.

Here we are at the gates,
Of the great and powerful Oz.

We'll gather en masse,
And we'll rip back the curtain because

There is evil afoot,
And we want a quick word
With the boss.

We've grown tired of his minions,
His rule, his bombs, and his lies,

And we're learning each day of his ways,
Cause it's time to get wise.

Of his patterns and plays which recur,
And are easy to spot.

Of his symbols and signs,
And subliminal, mindcheck garottes

Round the necks of humanity,
Cutting the heartspace clean off.

With media to hide what is real,
And project what is not.

So that what it was,
It wouldn't be,

And what it's not,
It would

You see?

The Return
Roseanna Kettle

We do love a crisis. These fortunate days,
These praise-singing days,
The plentiful hours
When corpsemeat's there to be had.

These desperate times
When all decorum disappears,
And grown men are so mad with fear
They'll point the finger anywhere,

And save for us the streets are bare.
Bright, and strangely clean,
No live unfathomable mess
Of human beings –

Just us – as usual,
We're dressed to the nines.
Scarce ever caught in the same skin twice,
Season to season, changing our stripes –

Hark, the return of primordial days!
The great rewilding – long epoch of peace!
Spread the word! – For we must purge disease.
You'll find that natural law agrees –

We scavengers-in-chief shall weigh
Whose life is for the reaping.
We hunger – and for blood we sing –
Who wants to die for a wished-for spring?

– No rush – we'll cull your stragglers
In time. But for the passing hour –
Aren't we dear, aren't we sweet,
As we swagger down your street?

Illustration © Helen Geddes

Sollicitum
Roseanna Kettle

Such drear news draws one in,
Freezes out the extremities,
Centres on the core.

I shrink from the light,
And as I have not done for years,
Enwreathe myself in it –

That knotty, selfish matter
Of the flesh,
Its constant revolt –

Thinking if I fear, and fear,
And feel the blow before it comes
It never will.

All this dwelling on imagined pains
And shying from real fear, why,
That's a fear in itself.

But who would court the whole ungoverned world
When I can hold a nightmare in my palm,
And fold it as I please?

Relapse
Roseanna Kettle

This incidence
Feels sharper than imagining,
Rivalling any before.

But, we two have lived through this,
And more,
The steely hum of my heart says.

I am the brilliant link
That holds you to being.
And now, how you rebuke me,

How readily forget –
Bedbound days of terror,
Friendless, seasick nights,

The whole frame run through
With anguish.
And yet you live. Still, I was there –

No more of this
Illusioned wallowing.
Don't turn from every injury that's past.

Each is a trophy, testament
To every time you fell,
Struck, to rise again.

What's come before
Is not to be sealed in the tomb,
But a torch, to the dark outstretched;

Bear it close to the breast.

Particles
Roseanna Kettle

Each
Irregularity
Spells out treachery,

And I stand hapless.
Made newly sensible
To a visionless world,
The frenzied wilderness
Alive on a finger's tip,
I am freshly afraid.

Such
Near undoing
Of all I hold to me,

Seems ever about to fall;
Tiny servants of being
The concreteness of life
Facilitate; Hands unseen
The visible world convey, and,
In a heart's beat, vanquish.

Cool,
Impassive
To the throes of materiality,

Such ever-present particles
Move, oblivious and mythic —
And yet, in every breathing.
In every home; the very fabric
Of a fragile body, near-divine,
In wait for deadly quickening.

Tableau Vivant
Roseanna Kettle

funny how
if I zero in,
I can summon it clear as sight,

shifting
and dreamlike, as in life.
and now – concentrate – suspend

the high glamour
of a voice familiar,
as if you now sung out to me –

elating.
I might charm you
to speak as I please,

picture it.
soon, the vision's complete.
you could stand manifest, enact

with soft words
any heartwarming scene,
with unadulterated vitality –

or, so it seems.
the original's fled,
the imitation stands without compare.

the after-image
haunts a dazzled eye,
usurps cold truth with untouchable light.

but who
can blame daydreamers
for chasing shadow-play,

when days rise ever
to a world unchanged,
though every heart should break –

mournless
I go on pretending,
no proper mantle screening you from
view,

nothing, save
the mind's unhallowed puppetry,
unhappy child of faultless memory.

Data Ghost
Roseanna Kettle

Grim though it seems,
There's no petty shame
In blotting out a sadness
To preserve some future day.

I would not be the soul
Who sups on sorrow,
Living for little more than death,
Turning mourning ever in its grave.

I should perish the thought,
Banish pain back
To its far frontier
To wait obedient

For a stray remembering.
But each digital movement,
As a wave, reaches
To dredge black litter from a distant shore,

The old face rises, fleshless –
Comes the carcass of some whitened wreck,
To grossly imitate
The seemingness of life.

I cannot make beautiful
Your absence, nor the lone
And spotless space
Where love once, enshrined, stood,

But I cannot block you out.
And so grief remembers itself,
Ever extant
In mesmeric light.

Seedlings
Roseanna Kettle

I've heard it said
That the turning of the trowel
In black earth, in search of fruit
Is a deep-dive,

Returning in new form
Memories long implanted,
Flowered by their re-knowing.
But, as I've no vernal expertise –

What is it, then, to set a seedling
In the bed, of misery sprung?
I did not, knowingly, imbue
This sickly sprout with heart and soul,

But sit tight for its blossoming –
I will it, swear there's meaning,
To invest in the soil my own living,
It's been said, to plant is to hope.

The capsule of this heartless time
Might, in temperate days, with patience,
Yield some kinder transformation,
Some delicious thing of worth.

God knows it must.

Wreath
Roseanna Kettle

when you and I walk out
you shall have all you desire,

blue hydrangea, any
chain of pinks serrated,
all roses' sickly splendour,
sprawling saxifraga,
laughing cinquefoil, delphinium too,
grave jasmine, baby's breath, the white
amaze of lilies; bind it up
together with ambrosial mimosae,
with it heavy love-lies-bleeding,
the trembling larkspur,
aramanth bejewelled, all
dizzying scents in one together blent,
aster, anemone, asphodel,
the osculant sweetpea –
the hyacinth that bleeds –
flowers never seen
by human eye, unimagined even –
why every gorgeous bower
that your proper soul deserves,

and with them all we'll walk
in perfect step.

Illustration © Helen Geddes

can you hear me
Isabel Head

if i could just hear your unfiltered v-

                          sorry hang on
              i think my signal's gone again
                    can you hear me

                            okay i said

i just want to hear your unfiltered voice
clear from the clogging of phone calls
and to see your face unpixellated
even if you were behind a pane of glass
i wouldn't have to touch you
just look at you from the other side
of a road and wave
knowing we were sharing some space
sharing some distance
for a moment

but we are very lucky and need to be grateful
for our chance to speak at all
either side of a phone call
still under each other's sky

                    oh
          did you not get any of that
      what was the last thing you heard me say

                 okay i just said
                     i just said

i miss you

pulling at threads
Isabel Head

not sure what to do
now i've finished this dress
perhaps i could pass the time by counting every stitch
do i count the one i got in my side on my
government sanctioned run
darn, maybe i zoned out while sewing
and tacked the fabric into my waist without noticing
maybe i should keep going, just to pass the time,
and sew my mouth shut with my last thread of patience
(does skin have a warp and weft)
that does seam a bit dramatic
for now, i'll pass the time trying to selvedge my sanity,
balanced on a needle point,
waiting for the tension to break

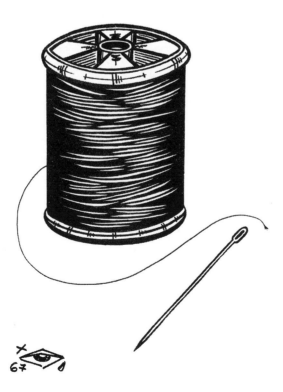

Illustration © HTH

Weaving
Anna Thornton

Wind-woven stems that coil,
flattened by 'work boots' and years'
roots that
have woven through
mangled shoots and
gowned grass and sunken soil. Weaving vines from
that past that spiral still
from summer-stained grass, still stroking the
spot where I sat heaving daisies from sleep-silent beds.
Chains of sunny-smiling heads,
and odd sheds of petals
sit knotted between pebbles on
the patio by rusting tools and tins of
screws.
Past's gate still creaks –
singing of careless entreats from
the blossom tree out on the front.
Each summer I'd hunt for the
whispers
that wove through every puncture
of broken sky,
through blotting of blossom's shade,

sun-white and wrinkled
behind weaving
pink-petaled wands. Brushing and frenzied
in flower, shaking embower, and showers
of sleet-coloured
confetti
collecting in
knotted blonde trails of hair.
I still sometimes find myself there,
unaware that awake, I desperately
shake the aged branches
which now break, instead of snowing
as they did.
Sagging-sad twigs,
since sunlight's touch left
the unkempt time of
songs that weave
like frost
through limpid-long grass,
and shine beyond that
expelled past.
Past the shed's broken glass –
and the creaking
still-song.

Illustration © Frances Sladen

Illustration © Robin Garside

Prosecco
Ray Hearne

Already distant history those first evenings
Bewildered March on its last legs loitering
Nothing seemed to suit but sitting out
Like awkward guests of our own little corner patch
Plant-pots. Wine-glasses. The fire-pit lit
Rough-headed beeches from the woods crowding in
Beyond them skyness
                              limitless ultramarine

Enlightening
Ray Hearne

Every night since, defying a wind's distemper
In this threadbare corner of the mother-tongue
Tying knots out of more mendacious pages
I have built my tiny wafer-thin iron-age hearth
As if there were gods still to be summoned, I'm chanting
Fire, flames and embers, even ash
At one with the face of heaven. Nothing flash.

The Four Walls of Quarantine
Ray Hearne

Years later as prisoners of the virus
The world outside became our exercise yard
A breather, borrowed from thrushes, snatched out of blossom
– rabid air rubbed our noses in it
Unlocked-down we felt, and lucky to be there
What saved us then was what will always save us
These flawed imaginations nature gave us

Thank you please
Ray Hearne

I'm staring at John Law's painting on my wall
The wateriest of sepia water-colours
Four Tommies in First World War tin hats, those 'Lions'
Following orders; ghosting off into oblivion.
On occasions, from the field beyond the secure unit
We are able now to hear donkeys braying
And health-workers toing, froing non-stop.
Just saying.

Black Lives Matter
Ray Hearne

All fenced in. Those manacles mind-forged still
Outside they're kneeling on our children's necks
In recent weeks we've strengthened our resolve
The flimsy artifice of hegemony
Glorifies malfunctioning apparatus
Nothing new in that to you and me
Or solidarity through poetry

Together
Tia Duff

Together we will remember
Not being allowed closer than 2m
FaceTime becoming the new normal
Distanced talks in the park

Together we will remember
The street erupting in applause on a Thursday evening
Staying inside to keep others safe
A family quiz on a Sunday night

Together we will remember
How much closer we all became
Weathering this storm from our individual boats
The kindness that came through all the pain

Illustration © Tia Duff

The Weeping
Jessie Summerhayes

Light plays with the dust on the ceiling –
steamy breath, the paint is peeling.
Sweeping heat – fingerprints weeping,
as they clutch at the rivulets – stare,
eyelash catching memories there,
shattered feelings sit in the lashes,
starlight creeps, funnelled by ashes,
black lines rim the edge of the water:
snaking inwards, darkened slaughter.
Dark blue room sleeping on the screen,
bottled water, truthful clean –
plastic corners creep unseen,
round the edges, my red porcelain heart –
fingernails peel – knuckles fall apart.
The hawthorn leaves toss in the night,
sleepless, dreaming of the white –
stretched paper, thin in the light.
Photograph blues with the ageing day,
crinkling smiles fade to the grey
of wolf. Driftwood sits in the lilac dark,
the islands whisper to the passing shark
of the seconds sleeping,
the weeping.

Illustration © Jessie Summerhayes

Islands Shout Shark
Jessie Summerhayes

Islands shout shark to the stars on the reef:
river chokes up – breathing teeth.
Dandelion clocks shatter all the windows,
creeping ivy – up the skin grows,
bony knuckles from the earth groan.
Sunlight burns the exposed white wall,
screens convulse, watching all:
memories tumble and crack.
Pounding skull resounding black.
Droplet resting on skin over bone,
spider legs snap – and tremble alone.
Body lodged in the dark of the stairs,
Wind selling a breath of air –
to the wet of the cheeks,
sweeps the sound of the voices,
choices, awash with fear,
into the screen – stark black and white,
moments swilling in the fight,
between reaching tide, grey hand –
golden arc, the beckoning sand.
Hinge it opens, the gaping maw –
blackness opens up before
the indefinite deep, the sinking ship,
narrow ever-numbing hips.
Wires slither on through the scum,
bedsheets saunter in the sun.

Ashen flies waltz round the light,
dust swims in the grovelling night
of the blood inside,
pounding at the veins – skin hides,
the yearning static rush of the heart
dormant seconds waiting to start
their crusade on the wooden chair,
ash settles on splintering seat,
glassy stare takes the least.
Blue light tendrils reach – suffocating,
breathing choking embracing –
windows steam, light it blurs –
whiteness reaches – towels concur.
Thread loosens at the seams of the lips,
water smothers our stagnant hips –
condensation carries the ships
white crescent moons
shape the flow,
water bends –
knuckles grow, engorged
with the power, eyesight distorts
in the wet of the shower
of thoughts that pummel the neck,
animating breaths you need to forget.
Windows weep as the splinters fall –
clicking keys sweeping all.
Detritus of life in a dustpan and brush,
cotton threads fray in the rush,
Islands shout shark to the stars on the reef:
river chokes up – breathing teeth.

Illustration © Jessie Summerhayes

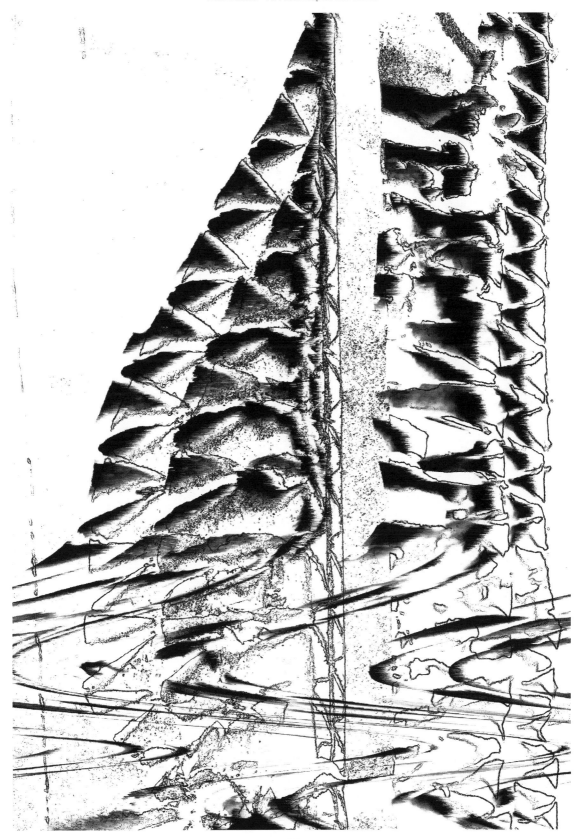

When Did We All Turn Green?
Jessie Summerhayes

Take your seconds back where you came from,
back to the screen and the pixels and
wait for the bananas to ripen and the tomatoes
beside them – perpetual injustice -
dried sweat on the neck – optimism wasted
on the square eyed sect and
the rest wait. Outcast. The plum tree
holds its breath and death closes
its eyes in surprise, as he is disregarded.
And the screen turns green for a new scene.
And the ten green bottles fall –
from the wall, all – smashed in our ignorance
of the light except the input chosen by those
who know, how to flow, the thoughts of
us and go from their seats to our heads in – know –
it doesn't matter, the chatter from the TV screen
observes truth,
and creates a youth,
who might be red but the bed matters more
than liberation and
you can use it to watch the world
go. Bye. Pixelated trees and the sky.
Watch with sinking eyes, blinking eyes,
watch the bananas moulder,
the plum tree falls and the ten green bottles
are smashed on the floor.
And perpetual injustice romps in our minds
so we look behind,
and the white wall stares and
the paper glares. Nobody cares.
Hours are moments
and eyes are the windows –
and that's where the screen goes,
staring back at me. And so, where did it go?
before the boat leaves surely
there's time to find myself, watching, up there on the shelf
flickers – then – eyes to the screen.
When did we all turn green.

Illustration © Jessie Summerhayes

Ode to Nigella
Jenny Knight

It is cold in this room
There's a strong smell of mould
It's the best I can get
Nothing for me, I'm told.
I'm a carer, for those
Who are struggling so,
Who can't care for themselves,
My salary's low.
Can't afford my own place
So I'm renting this room
Keeping warm in my bed.
Nigella's on soon.

She has left her big house
In London somewhere
She will drive her posh car
To get some fresh air
In the country, her place
With a barn – she must rest
She needs a martini
Some 'me time'. She's stressed.

She'll make twinkly biscuits
For when people drop in
She'll make twinkly cocktails
With top quality gin
She will smirk at the camera
She'll whisk and she'll cut
She'll do double entendres
It'll never be smut.
She will devil her eggs
Pomegranate it up
She will look on her shelves
For a suitable cup
Or a bowl or a spice
Or a whisk or a sauce
She'll mix lots of things up
(Copper mixer, of course)
Then her 'friends' will arrive
Under twinkling lights
And flickering candles
The table delights.

It is cold in this room
There's a strong smell of mould
I'm a carer, you see,
For the sick and the old.

Illustration © Bryan Ledgard

Breathing
Jenny Knight

Explain to me, please, why we're laying the wreaths
For the people who left us, unable to breathe
Wreaths lie by buildings – wreaths lean on walls
In front of the crowds, in front of us all.

Explain to me why we are losing our breath
As we fall to one knee, as we witness more death
As the innocent die and the sickness spreads fast
As the effigies fall and we gasp at our past.

There's a gasp of the fight and a sigh in our flight
And a sharp grasp at air to scream out in the night
For a light, for a nurse, for some kindness, some good
To unravel the things we thought we understood.

We are wrong, we are right, we are living in death
We are good, we are bad, we are gasping for breath
In a moment in time when so much time is spare
Altogether alone. We are going nowhere

Breathe in and breathe out, deeply, through the nose
This cycle of motion and then of repose
Use the diaphragm, don't use the chest, so they say
But we're choked by our tears so can't breathe anyway

The rhythm is broken. Each breath runs into the next
Breath, as we learn the pain of no breath,
And we watch as he begs for his chance to inhale
And we watch her turned over – her lungs fit to fail.

Universal, this thing. Life in motion as one
All breathe in then breathe out then the break has to come
If it starts it will stop, if it comes it will go
Where there's bad there is good. That's all we'll ever know.

So take in some air, sing a love song for all
A protest with love, take the wreaths from the wall
There's more than one virus ... in each of us death
And the end is always our one final breath.

Illustration © Mel Ledgard

Virtual Purgatory
Jenny Knight

It's a Microsoft Teams meeting day
Eleven o'clock we all chat
I've put on a top that's been ironed
Shut the door too, to keep out the cat.
There's a room in my house full of books
It would seem that's the place I should be
Check the books first, of course – no self help.
I've been studying it all on TV.

We've decided that we should all 'meet'
To make strategic plans, and catch up
For when "all this is over" (no dates)
I've made coffee in my Fortnum's cup.
Some have cameras on. Others prefer
To just listen behind a grey square
If they don't speak it starts to feel weird
And you wonder if they're really there.

But the colleagues you see set the tone
Sitting upright, and looking quite keen
Doing nodding and listening heads
(Slightly tilted). Gazing at the screen.
Subject matter, as usual, banal
Made more tedious as we navigate
Taking turns, making sure we feel 'heard',
Awkward silences. Points made too late.

Someone's doorbell has rung. Off she goes
(Dodgy shorts on. And slippers! Who knew?)
We all wait in our boxes until
She comes back. And she says "72
Hours to leave it". A murmur is heard,
Of agreement, just laced with self-doubt
We all know we've torn open our parcels
Too soon for the germs to die out.

I enjoyed that bit more than the rest.
Haven't seen her in slippers before
She looked smart from the waist up of course.
Note to self: always plan for the door.
Anyway, we've been here for an hour
Talking crap in such business like ways
And I think there's a vibe coming through
That we'd like to get on with our days.

Someone's asked me a question on teams
I admit that my mind was elsewhere
I caught sight of my books on the screen
And my '50 shades' book is still there!
It was tucked between Shakespeare and Fromm
Hadn't noticed it until today
I honestly thought that my hair
Was the one place to see shades of grey.

Need the doorbell to ring – Amazon
Need the cat to be sick in the hall
Need a call from someone – 'phone for you'
Need to wrap this up once and for all
I should never have plumped for the books
And the lighting's too harsh in this room
I'll rethink things for later today
When we 'meet' for the quiz night on Zoom.

Illustration © Ian Meade

Before
Jane Hilberry

It's not as though I was gorging on kisses,
the daily bread of sex, before the governor told us
to stay home. It's not as if grandchildren piled

into bed with me in the mornings begging
to visit the horses that live – oddly – at the edge
of the apartment complex. In truth,

I'd come home and drop my keys,
feed the cat, eat something myself –
sink into the couch & click on tv.

It's not what I hear people say –
"I miss hugs" –
which annoys me somehow.

But now when students mute themselves,
I can't hear the always-late kid
scrape his chair up to the table, unwrap

the egg and bagel that I can't smell –
can't hear the all the pencils scrubbing
the page, hair falling into their eyes.

It was all a form of touch.
Kara arranging snacks for the meeting.
Dez's laugh, clip of Jessica's clogs,

heading out to walk Finn. And Seth,
who is there like the earth itself.
Am I writing a love letter to my workplace?

My office is calm, painted green, but everyone
has a key. What I mean is that someday
worms will enter my body, no difference

between me and everything else,
the coffin a formality, an idea of a boundary.
I miss being no different, breeze

coming through the screen, voices of students
kicking a ball on the quad, four-year-olds
running to pick flavors at the Sno-Cone truck.

I'm alone in bed, reading. The spring wind shifts.
I can almost hear buds forming and opening.
My mind's on edge. It might just crack

if I can't walk toward someone.

Technophobe
Lee Baskerville

Texting, sexting,
I find it quite perplexing
Pmsl, lol and rotflmao as well
Snapchat, then there's Kik
Available in just 1 click.

Texting, sexting,
Positively vexing
Grindr, Tinder, come and meet Melinda!
Online dating
It ends up quite deflating.

Texting, sexting,
Attracting either sex in
Assignations, abbreviations
Only give me palpitations.

Texting, sexting,
Index fingers flexing
All this could be good. Right?
Or am I just a Luddite?

Texting, sexting,
I wonder what's the next thing?
Takes such effort. It's demanding.
I don't like not understanding!!

Lockdown Breakdown
(or Reflections In A Flat)
Lee Baskerville

It's hard to find positives amidst this global malaise
I can't get any baked beans, and I've been stuck in for days
All the doctors and nurses deserve a huge raise
And shop workers, lorry drivers and carers our praise.

The Government and experts have guidance to impart
Please stay at home, think of others, be smart
Social distancing means keeping 2 metres apart
But I did imperial, so that's a bugger for a start!

But back to the positives, look and you will find
Folk in our communities being incredibly kind
So our elderly and vulnerable aren't left behind
By fetching their shopping and nobody minds.

You're starting to look what's at the back of the cupboard
Cos the supermarket shelves look like Mother Hubbard's
You're dining on stuff you haven't tried for years
Like cannelloni beans with asparagus spears.

Drinking at home can be a bit of a bind
But the advantage, of course is there's no closing time
Mind, the post drinkie supper is a little bit boring
Sat up all night with a celery stick, gnawing.

The nation tunes into the briefing at five
To see how many of the populace are still alive
The horror of it all plays out before our eyes
Yet we're becoming immune, it's no great surprise.

There's no sport being played in any competition
Matt Hancock speaks of footballers with derision
Yep, all competitions have been suspended
Even golf, it's a case of Open, ended.

All non essential businesses have been forced to close
The Government had no real choice I suppose
And those staying open – a monumental task
Keeping us apart from behind a face mask.

Social media is alive with feel good content
That sees the pathos and fun, and not the portent
Online gigs, untapped songwriting skills
New friends and connections, a Facebook of thrills.

Virtual Slimming World and exercise regimes
By a hunk bedecked in Lycra extreme
My wife says this lockdown's not as bad as it seems
Being told how to flex by the man of my dreams.

I seem to spend all day staring at tomes
On bookcase backdrops from interviewee's homes
Inertia is causing my body and brain to cramp up
Politicians don't 'increase' anymore, cos everything's ramped up.

Jobsworths coming out of the woodwork like worms
Enforcing spurious essential purchasing terms
Two genuine examples that I've known come to hand
M&S knickers and lottery tickets – BANNED!

But if we all act responsibly and stay in it together
This lockdown and virus crisis won't last forever
And we can rid ourselves of a world getting sillier
And return to normality and something more familiar.

Starling Dance
David Weir

Birds swarm over Runcorn Bridge, spraying up over the high girders
Bare in the evening afterglow, night club plasma mottling an evening wall.
High twisting in the arms of steel these dancers thrill the evening clouds
Tangoing swirls reversing, leaders alternating, rhythms pulsing.
Close-combined, never touching, as one cloth, murmurating.
A hidden conjuror whirling a shimmering sheet across winter clouds.
As dark closes the show, curtains fall over Mersey.
A million-speckled shawl settles into wetlands.
Our car has moved on a mile nearer home.
We, journeying millennia, still travelling.
All quiet now.

Journeyman
David Weir

Journeyman in his overalls walking up Long Field
Catching a foot uneasy against the stubble
Taking a long short-cut, back to a real day
Before machines reduced this corn
To a carpet-even nine inch cut.

Teams of twenty, men, boys, and old'uns
Followed reaper and binder up Long Field
Up the uneven rows of sheaves,
Knocking the heads to start the stooks
Picking razor-sharp spines from bloody fingers
Cussing at steady pace.
Stooks, like Indian tents of gold
Small temples of plenty,
Marked men's duty, achieved in Long Field .

Days punctuate with morning 'lowance
Dinner of four pies, two fruit, two tasty
Afternoon 'lowance, small beer sometimes..
The sweet solemn impertinence of pipe baccy,
Incense offerings of men's afternoon pleasure,
Curling upwards to greet the on-coming evening.

That was a field to walk in then.
Men strode it then together.
Long slow jokes, football and girls
Days past and days to come
Part of a common pattern.

Now one old man stumbles
On machine-regular obstacles
Walls of exclusion against man's need
To feel his earth.
Only one of us left now, journeyman.
Sad work today in Long Field.

Bovine Social Spacing
David Weir

Ploughed field dips to a wooded fence
A dozen cows huddle, but what against?
No wind scouring, no snow falling
No farmer coming, and why not closer to shelter?
At twenty paces, one cow sits alone.
Some puzzles, then, theirs and ours.
Do cows decide where to sit?
Are minority views allowed?
And which of them will ever tell us?
The herd or the loner? Who's talking?
Or do we know already, somewhere
Deep hidden under words?

Illustration © Bryan Ledgard

Home
Natalie Saturnia

My grandmother's pendant hangs heavily
upon my neck; I feel my tiny hairs
caught in the gold chain like woodlice.
Each pinprick that reminds me of her presence,
tells me equally of her loss.

My home is a half-melted candle;
too special to burn,
a book whose spine I have cracked
until it turned white with ache,
my grandad's tobacco pouch,
weathered and worn.

I cling to this idea of stability
And like a precious painting
I grasp it tightly in my fists,
desperate not to lose it,
my knuckles turning white with resolve.

Blinded by my own desperation,
I am naïve to the oils in my hands
eroding the image,
my fingernails becoming slick
with paint,
black and blue.

Illustration © Ian Meade

Sunray
Natalie Saturnia

In my dreams, the sun glistens on my skin,
and a kestrel warms my ears,
her golden beak nuzzling against my cheek.
I hold nature tightly in my fist,
all of Earth's greenery seems the size of a pinkie nail:
petite, unflinching, mine.

At dawn, I am pulled from my bed,
a submissive magnet to the sun.
No matter how rooted to the mattress
my bones swear they are,
I am made merciless and malleable
by the certainty that the sun will rise and set again.

I am a sunray
burning too hot for my own good,
ignited in an instant by a sharp word,
brought to tears by the passing
of plucked flowers in my room.

At night, my breaths harmonise
with the ocean's heartbeat,
and the continents move beneath my feet.
I see myself from the sun's point of view:
small and pink, as fragile as a calf,
suspended in the benevolence of Earth's wing.

Turning Point
Francesca Lea

We dwarf yet we should be dwarfed,
In a world of 7 billion,
Of constant bustle, and out loud cries,
We work out of sync and rhythm.

Hidden within noise, we sleep out of tune,
Competing against no competition,
It is, almost too late to realise,
Our domination is our mission.

The birds hover above the horizon,
Exposed to nature, gliding and glistening,
Yet our success has become our failure,
Cars that shield and conceal, a partition.

We have drowned the outside, with washed out noise,
Making our presence inescapable,
Our tempo is fastening, quickening,
The current lifestyle is unstable, unobtainable.

The chain falls, string sprung, and thread broken,
A solution with no answer, our tempo slows.
The ringing alarm and bell has spoken …
We restart to a new lifestyle imposed.

We cannot but hear the morning birds sound,
Exposed to the outside heartbeat and rhythm,
Unified, beautified, preoccupied,
We live in surround sound and high definition.

Twittering and humming fill our ears,
We cycle in harmony and rhythm,
Sustaining a tempo, to switch gears,
We have now created an in-sync vision.

Thoughts Of The Past, In Isolation
John Law

You find, with pain, that you are 'at risk' because now, you are old.
The years have flown by to this, leaving marks of joy and pain
And remembrance.

Lost friends; lost loves; lost dreams teem in your mind.
Though things once important have faded to a dim recollection,
Lost in a mist.

The trivial and the fleeting now weigh heavily on your thoughts;
A word spoken in haste long since, that hurt a friend, now
Cannot be forgotten.

Those lost summers of youth, live again, in sun and flowers,
Old lovers return to mind, faces unchanged by the bridge of years,
Smiling once again.

Young folk of today, confident and careless, ignore the warnings.
Not caring that their future grows shorter while their past,
Grows longer every day.

Remember your happy times, look back with joy and love,
At that which cannot come again. We are isolated, but the past remains
For those to see, that will.

Illustration © John Law

Remember
John Law

Games we played in gangs and teams,
Full of life and joy and screams.
Tin-can telephones, joined with string.
Throwing arrows were the thing.
Nails squashed flat upon the track,
Boomerangs that won't come back.
Kick-can, hop-scotch, whip and top,
Games we thought would never stop.
Snobs and Sticks, King of the Pile.
At school we walked in crocodile.
Marbles, flick-cards we would fight,
Clicking frogs, Mischievous Night.

'Husty, busty, finger, thumb, a dum or Little Granny'.

Jubblies; kali; arrowroot rock;
Liquorice root and Rainbow Drops.
Mojos; Lucky Bags and Imps,
Dolly Mixtures; Penny Shrimps.
Sweet cigarettes and Sherbet Dips;
Chocolate Mice and Cherry Lips.
For Fry's 5 Boys we all would wish,
Traffic light lollies and spice fish.
Sour Grapes; Swizzells and spanish
All our pocket-money vanished
Highland Toffee; Flying Saucers;
Gobstoppers and chocolate horses.

*'A finger of Fudge is just enough to give your
kids a treat.'*

Catty strags and acorn pipes;
Dastering and Mam's spit-wipes.
Social on a Friday night;
Trolleys and newspaper kites.
Dams and frog-spawn; spud-guns; smoke;
Segs and Christmas cracker jokes.
Rowntree's Gollies, gone for good;

Pop can-openers; Nobbies pond mud.
Dan Dare badges; first ink pen;
Brylcreem machine; inkwells; dens.
Turnip lanterns; skull rings; newt;
Conkers; alleys; what a beaut!

'Colman's Mustard, Colman's Starch,
Tell Mr Colman to shove it up his arse.'

Nit-nurse; rag-and-bone man; caps;
Brilliantine and Brigger's axe.
Mrs Wright's and Ivor's chippy
37 bus and Clippie.
Melting lead in old tin-cans.
Pie and Pea van; Pig-swill Man.
Pea-shooters made of Mother-die.
Handyshop; you made me cry.
WRCC bog-roll;
Dansette record players; Joel;
Back and forth his house to mine,
Sun Mist bike, the weather's fine.

'It's Friday, it's five-to-five, it's – CRACKERJACK'.

Things we read; watched; listened then:
Captain Pugwash; Flowerpotmen.
Watch with Mother; Doctor Who;
Johnny Morris at the zoo.
Woodentops and Andy Pandy
Beezer; Topper; Beano; Dandy.
Funny programmes filled with mirth
'My-hi name is Harry Worth'
405 lines; Interlude;
Blue Peter Badges; bog-roll tube.
Outer Limits; Twilight Zone,
Magpie; Daleks; white-spot tone.

'WE HAVE TAKEN CONTROL OF YOUR SET'.

Club
John Law

Bright and smoky, pound-a-pint din.
Old men sitting, false teeth grin.
Blue smoke, blue scars, pit-reminder.
Doms and cribbage, played a blinder.
Blue suit jacket, brown keks half-mast,
Showing socks: once new, long past.
Fair Isle jumpers, belt and braces.
Kicking over old men's traces.

Horse race, cricket, snooker, football.
Facts and figures, total recall.
Who won what, who scored, who missed.
Who lost, who found, who smacked, who kissed.
Times gone by, the present banished.
Lost in talk of times long-vanished.
Miner's Monday, club-trips, Leger.
Blackpool Race-week, rainy weather.

Best Room, half-of-lager, fags.
Wives and girlfriends, clutch handbags.
Lipstick reddened, perfumed and scrubbed,
Saturday night out in the club.

All that matters is the chatter,
See the reputations shatter.
That and Bingo makes the night,
Everything turns out alright.

Two Fat Ladies, clickety-click,
Lines are filling, feeling sick.
Pull-it! pull-it! will it come?
Ten-pound house, a tidy sum.
Pay the milkman, Seaside ride.
"Here" from over t'other side.
Disappointment fills the air,
Next house maybe, I'll be there.

Last orders gone, turn is done.
Last house played, time has come.
Cold night air, breathe like mist.
Chip-shop calling, all well pissed.
Fish and peas with bits on top,
Salt and vinegar, can of pop.
Replayed, unchanging, year on year,
But for the rising price of beer.

Illustration © Dave Howarth

Summer Sunday
John Law

Ice-cream man, Danny's van.
Summer swelter, tar-melter.
Hop-scotch square, do or dare.
Cricket crease, go-kart grease.
Bird's nest found, walking round.
Climbing trees, scabby knees.
Nobby's pond, bulrush frond.
Cold frog spawn, my front lawn.
XL5, Juke box jive.
Thunderbirds, lemon curd.
Playing out, Mother's shout.
Coming home – not alone.
Noise and din, running in.
Daddy's there, combing hair.
Wireless plays, summer days.
Sunday night, golden light.
Feeling glad, watching Dad.
Hear the song, evening long.
"Sing Something Simple, as cares go by.
Sing Something Simple, just you and I." [1]

---

[1] *Theme from* Sing Something Simple. *BBC Radio Light Programme and Radio 2. Attributed to Cliff Adams. The programme became the longest continuously running music programme in the world from 1959 until 2001.*

There is a Dangerous Man on the Loose
Sophie Norton

Picture COVID-19 as a
megalomaniac wack-job. Your
neighbourhood loony bin.
A
hypothetical
farce-show
who says no
to the conglomerate of companies that are after
our money. He stops the roads and staggers
around,
spewing pestilence
for the needy. He
feels like a dream,
a slipstream.
A disappointed PVC-slapped
jumbo sticker on the back of a
confederate masterpiece. The
laws of physics don't apply
here, suddenly everyone's
unnamed
and untamed
in a computer
simulation game
where the aim to
stay alive
is to remain inside.

Quarantine is a Circus
Sophie Norton

It feels like we're waiting in line for a joyride but the line is a carnival and the car is a circus tent. Your birthday is a live action performance and the lion is tired of his predicament.

Surprise!! The ostentatious freaks from South Carolina want to be our friends but we can't hug them so what's the point in trying?

You licked my hand through a latex glove and I felt the crowd applaud. Merriment doesn't make money, the box office does but we can't pay the rent if all our actresses are on minimum wage. Shadows don't fall from grace, it's the cyclists and tightrope walkers that suffer. Smoke screens without coloured lights are just accidents waiting to happen.

You can run from the fortune teller's tent into a dandelion but ain't nothin gonna make that wish come true. The spotlight's on a specific clown but we've all heard his story before.

Uncle Rubert takes a suitcase from the bandstand and there's sawdust in my shoe from the elephant parade. The dancers from Act 5 are intimidated by your facial expressions but the show must go on.

The ensemble is a pandemic and the remedy is the small quantity of popcorn that may be purchased from the front desk during the intervals. Lights are up and everyone's leaving. A child has left their shoe in one of the front stalls but hope is not lost because although it can be retrieved by the caretaker, this circus sure isn't returning anytime soon.

Illustration © Paul Gough

The Wind

Cyang Stifano

Looking out of my window yesterday
I was trying to connect with the wind.

With the sound of the breeze and the sun hitting my legs, the warmth that gave
me. Through the double glazed glass you could still imagine you are out there,
that you can have a bit of freedom, even if it's not true just a product of our
imagination, but man, it feels real.

Sitting there, trying to remember what was it like to just go on about your day
without having to do much thinking, these days have made me realise, how
complicated our minds can be: well, don't get me wrong, I've always known
that, we are just so used to ignoring it.

That we forget.
We forget how to live.

Because everything seems to be planned for us …
already constructed
organised.

My days have now come down to looking out, asking questions, trying to find
the answers, not fully knowing they are not there.

It's not external: we already know them.

Illustration © Stephen Cox

Drive-by lives
Chloe D'Arcy

Drive-by lives wave to us through glass,
as we wait for the day we'll breathe and
taste untainted air, and drink from Lethe
to forget pacing purgatory. We'll bypass
fear: the glaring omens of its neon flashes,
its siren's cries which keep us hidden,
as we weep for worlds long forbidden.
For when we, addled and grey, may return
at last to mass and kneel, we'll commend the
lost and fallen, those present and spirits
passed. So, we'll wait.

Fishbowl
Chloe D'Arcy

Drifting through silent streets,
distant coughs startle
emboldened birds, a fox's shadow
in the light of a shop-
front steps into nonexistence
and the man in his fishbowl
living room is gone

Somewhere white and
sterile, away from the hub
bub of Coronation Street
and reminiscing about the
people who used to board and
alight the bus outside,
smiling at him from time to
time, but like ghosts now
filter rarely by.

Illustration © Howard Aynhoe

Encore
(Dedicated to the Tyne Theatre & Opera House, Newcastle-upon-Tyne)
Jenni Pascoe

We will keep your memories safe.
We will hold on to your spark.
We are your ghost lights, sharing
starry glimmers through the dark.
Your play has not yet ended –
This is just a script rewrite.
A stage you're going through
in your long, dramatic life.
When the scene finally changes,
we will raise your curtain high.
And raise a glass to your next act –
With love from your Team Tyne.

Gratitude
Jenni Pascoe

Imagine this with no internet
Imagine this with no NHS
Imagine this without a phone
Imagine this without a home
It might be tough, but could be much worse
Be grateful for each and every nurse
Be grateful you are still connected
Be grateful if you're not infected
Be kind, we can beat this, and when we do
Remember the people who got us through

Metamorphosis
Jenni Pascoe

Chrysalis distanced
Alone we are united
Butterflies will rise

Illustration © Jed Grimes

Plague poems
Liz Deakin

Number 1

Yesterday in the hour before the pool closed
I swam alone, safe, in my chlorine ocean.
Now, on the far side of the mirror..
all closed.. all gone..shut-in..shut-out..
days..months..years..
within a virtual crowd
some embracing their Anchorite life
while others strip supermarket shelves.
A few, like me, walk by the waves
here in Stalingrad-on-Sea.

Number 2

Although Pall Mall caravan site is closed
it proudly flew St George's flag
till Welsh Nat Steve-With-The-Green-Hair slashed it.

A first death in Aberdyfi they say
And another in Pennal.

Tywyn High Street, apocalypse bare,
echoes to the steps of those scurrying to their burrows.
In the afternoon we trudge through sandhills above a grey sea –
later, listen to dispatches from the front line.
I read another chapter of *The Plague Dogs* by Richard Adams
as one more *long day's journey into night* closes

Number 3

Now the streets, empty, silent.
A shrouded woman posting a letter,
petrified by our approach,
scuttles across the road.

We walk along Faenol Isaf
past posh houses
where a pair of outraged geese
hiss and shriek at our intrusion.

On through a copse,
Over a rickety stile
Through a muddy field
Across the railway line
Through a farmyard
where hearty walkers greet us
without fear.

We emerge on the Aberdyfi road
above the health centre car park
normally so full
but now it waits, empty,
like the hushed town,
for the dreaded peak.

Number 4

Like Crusoe this dismal morning
reading footprints in the sand –
heavy, light, runners' deep gashes,
big and little paw prints of romping dogs
defying their seasonal exclusion.
Above, on the prom,
the electric whine and clatter of invalid carriages
speeding by
as the expected rain begins.

continued overleaf …

Number 5

We misread the tables
and too soon scrambled to rescue towel and shoes
from the sweeping tide.

Disgruntled, we lingered on the steps
winkling wet sand from our toes.

Startled by the dreadful noise of a sneeze,
we looked upwards into a wild face
leering at us over the promenade wall

So … has our growing obedience to the rules
our participation in the engulfing fear
been in vain?

Has one man's spite
one man's vengeful misery
penetrated the armour of our comfortable respectability?

We must wait and see

Number 6

Tomorrow and tomorrow and tomorrow
Why bother? – it's all been said
As daylight lingers, my days shorten –
So busy doing nothing.
Vaguely I contemplate *The Lotus Eaters* and my navel
A land where all things always seemed the same.
Dutifully I plod by the sea
A corn nags between my toes and distant dolphins
leaping in the bay, fail to raise my spirits.
Others point and marvel
As cars disgorge excited strangers
To trespass on my melancholy.

Illustration © Liz Deakin

Coronavirus
Maurice Rutherford

I'm now grown old, and have no hair to comb,
no wife to chide me when I fall asleep.
The over-seventies should stay at home,
we're told. I'm in my nineties – in them deep,
so where does that place me? Should I be caged,
handcuffed and ostracized for having aged?
Please watch the Covid updates on TV
and warn me of the fate in store for me.

Illustration © Jeannie Clarke

Jeannie Clarke

Jeannie Clarke

Lockdown Lunches
Maurice Rutherford

Almost two lost months,
or sixty times lunch alone,
or a whole case or more
of fine Australian wine,
or however you'd care
to measure these slow-go days
since the pleasure of vintage
company at lunch was mine.

How steeply I have slipped
down the decorum scale
to a loll-about Yankee style:
food chopped small on the plate,
my fork a shovel dangling
from one lazy hand, head cradled
in the other, elbow to table.
Slob, with an indolent gob.

Can this, then, be me?
'Haikuist, I'm bound to say
"Yes", disgustedly!

Illustration © Jeannie Clarke

Northern Exposure
Stephen Linstead

There's barren distance now,
A dismal silence edging between us and growing like a glacier,
But huddling against the chill last night
Our bodies murmured a little last warmth.
Unmoving, gentle skin communication held us.
Now, bitten by the crisp air
Beneath the cold stone of the field wall shading it
Ribs gaping skyward
Fat glistening on flesh-picked bones
Amid the dry parched remains of some days' meals
The eyeless staring skeleton grins at me
In solitary communion.
It has been dead some time,
But the stripping of the joints has barely ceased.
A whole carcass, strewn and partially dismembered,
Almost a full grown sheep, but now
A few errant grafted tufts of wool that don't yet
Line nests are scattered among the couch grass.
Shivering Spring birds gingerly spread a halting canopy of song.
The early morning sun insinuates warmth
But the wind whips sinfully over the chilled slopes.
Life lumbers on.
I glance to the small grey graveyard on the eastern lee
Where families ruefully struggle among themselves to lie
Beneath the white church wall
Whilst beyond that bitter hill in the grey graveyard of the bruised living
They struggle among themselves to live.
There as here, they will have their pickings
And the dying may not be swift
But all will go, all utterly consumed.
Tarn bred, this stubborn land
Dessicates my words,
Forces me to sheathe my metaphors
And turn my shadowed face to where a sullen sun
Might yet glance a gritty beam.

Illustration © Aneta Horodecka-Kwiatek/Mark K Allen

The Prospect Behind Us
Stephen Linstead

Like a pantomime villain
Or hoodied mugger
Our future is behind us
Creeping up unseen
Beladen with chickens
Coming home to roost
Bulging briefcases of dog-eared
Accounts to be reckoned with
Beneficent sacks of serendipity
And whatever's coming to us.

Whichever direction we look in
The traumatic thaumaturge
Is always behind us
Whilst the pantomime audiences of history
Scream hysterical indecipherable warnings
As our befuddled faces peer.
It has no reflection in life's rear view mirror
And never shows up on our mindless selfies
Of self-consciousness.

We don't back away from the future
We just back into it
And when it arrives
We deny that the ships have come in
Or pretend that the tawdry eagles have landed
With feathers intact
Or try to send it packing
With ears full of exhausted fleas
Whilst we gaze into the hollows
Of the dark auditorium
Struggling to perceive what hides in past light.

And if through shifting scenes
We nimbly avoid fate's sudden trapdoor
We can't slink off into the wings
Unanchored by its haunting shadow
Or the gelled light that leaks
Fuzzily focused from out of frame.
We can't step forward beyond proscenium play
Into knowledge.

For all our props and make-up
Idiots' tales and pyrotechnics
We are puppets without strings
And always, ever, becoming from behind.

Illustration © Barry Fox

Desert Meditation 1: Saguaro
Stephen Linstead

Sometimes like a man, sometimes twisted
Like the burden of others' expectations
Taller than houses, older than trees
This is your scorching land.
You don't want another.
Even where the air is dry and the land parched as this
You scorn to cross that line
And remain to give life to this flat-scrubbed rock.
In this desert there is life
When saguaro feels the knife.
Water your gift, timber for shelter,
Your lessons endure the silent swelter.
Among the bones, the scuttling lizards
Disappear in the heat.
Dry skin cracks in a smile's width
As the sweat's salt makes me smart.
Stones teach me to be at one with this.
Show me the life in this death
Better to see the death of life in
Street-smart boutique-chic critique.
The earth-bound tree-huggers of Las Cruces
Shunned this sharper, seeping succulent.
But with blossom-beaked hummingbirds I share its sin,
And the sweet taste of its bitter wisdom

Illustration © Aneta Horodecka-Kwiatek/Mark K Allen

Standing tall...
Eth Holmes

Stand in strength,
though I am weary,
but in doubt I will not fall,
and if you take me, do it quickly,
for still, I will stand tall.

Strip my flesh
and crush my bones,
see me bleed and hear me weep,
but not once, will my head bow,
despite all this, I will stand tall.

Take my heart
and lay it bare,
wreck my life if you so care,
but my heart will never vary,
as its strength will keep me tall.

Tear my soul,
shred it to pieces,
strip my heart, cleave it in two,
my depth of spirit will outwit you,
and I will stand, forever tall.

Illustration: 'Charlotte and the Hands of Fatima guard McKinley's Soul' © Anne Genner Crawford

Sweet Comfort
Eth Holmes

I close my eyes and dream a dream
of strangers so unknown to me
that float within my silent nights
and tell me things I've never heard.
They edge themselves up close to me,
engulf me in their mystery,
its then I close my eyes again
tight shut, tight shut,
they hold me there.

Within my thoughts within my mind,
no longer blind
to whispers in my psyche and soul,
these people softly call.
Those whispers through subconscious thought,
they tell me things they think they ought,
and show me faded avenues
obscured behind such secrecy,
through windowed worlds unknown to me,
all shrouded in great mystery.
I close my eyes
tight shut, tight shut
they hold me there
and comfort me,
I sleep.

Illustration: 'Dark Fable' © John A McPake

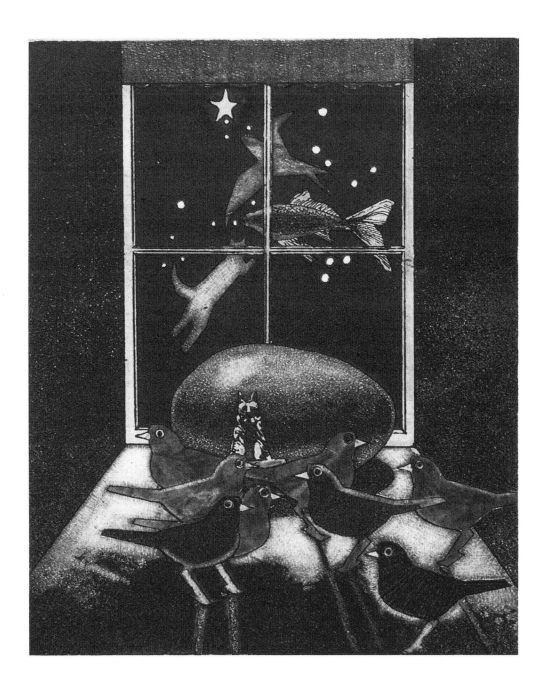

Haiku sequence, Spring 2020
Laura Potts

"I wrote a first daily haiku sequence when I was staying on Colonsay in the Hebrides, one of my favourite places to be. I liked the discipline of distilling a day into 17 syllables, refining what were the significant observations and feelings. So it seemed a way of containing the suddenly formless and confusing times of the pandemic, which coincided with the emergence of spring; noticing nature and change are features of many classical Japanese haiku. This series runs from just before the equinox to the solstice. The other element of this series is my mother's continuing decline from dementia in a local care home, while I have been unable to visit her. And I've had many cycle rides out of town through this period, longing for space and distant horizons."

Illustration: 'Colonsay Moon' © Bryan Ledgard

March 20th EQUINOX
Lurch of night time fear.
A tally of hugs in store.
Dark clouds; bright spring sun.

April 1st
Rowan leaves open.
Moments of normality.
Then the school clock stops.

April 7th
Fracturing chaos.
Against the order of seed
Sowing in the sun.

May 11th
There's a frost that kills.
We are told to stay alert,
While they flounder on.

June 3rd
A stop and a shift:
We've come to revolution.
There's no going back.

We are the Grandparents
Carina Riley

We are the Grandparents, the top of the tree.
We are meant to see what the young ones can't see.
We've lived the life, we've walked the path.
We show them when to cry, and when they should laugh.
We are the knowledge, the 'I told you so!'
We are the light showing which way to go.
But this time is different, this time is new.
This time we don't know what we should do.
How can we guide them?
We can't see the way.
How can we hold them?
When they're far away.
Now we are equal in life and in death,
Now we are sharing the same frightened breath.
So here in our bubbles we self isolate,
They wave and leave parcels for us by the gate.
We all rely on people that we may never meet,
We share our thanks stood clapping in the street.
So we are the Grandparents and we hold our love tight,
For family and friends, when the world is put right.

I wrote this one night when I couldn't sleep.

Illustration © Stephen Cox

Ssh, Don't Say a Word
David Driver

Soaking in the silence, soothed by the calmness, the sunshine and a gentle breeze
blowing lightly on my face

Bushes bloom, bearing berries which feed my feathered friends. I close my eyes
and birdsong takes me to happy memories

Dragonflies hover over a summer pond and fish lightly break the surface, talking
in bubbles of silent speech

A red kite soars on advantageous thermals searching for a lazy hare lost in
dreams.

Swallows swoop, gulping from the water of canals, whilst mallards rest at ease
on the far side away from the worn boots of ramblers which have clocked up a
thousand miles.

Ssh, don't say a word.

Illustration © Bryan Ledgard

Four New Friends
David Driver

Within these four walls I've made four new friends
Catching up on the gossip, making amends
Drowning on dry land, a diver without the bends

A twenty first century Ben Gun, let me out please
I'm fed up with eating tinned spam and I really don't like cheese
Imprisoned in my living room and a blind jailer holds the keys

UK Gold with Bergerac
Beans on toast and a pack of Caramac
When this is over I'm sending my Sky Box back

Five card stud, but no one's dealing
Your face is cracked and your clothes are peeling
By not answering my questions my sanity you're stealing

We're The Magnificent Seven, including ceiling and floor
But wait a minute, window wants to join us and so does door
Please play nicely, I can't take anymore

A human goldfish going around in my own living room
There's no point broadcasting the weather, it's all doom and gloom
Insanity season and the madness is in bloom

Lockdown
David Driver

Boris has spoken, all have heard
Stay inside people, penalties may be incurred

Locked within four walls, like a trapped mouse
Bricks, mortar, a roof, it's called your house

Paint the walls, or try some tiling
Office workers don't worry, the socks need filing

Monopoly, Kerplunk are both board games
Yes these are your kids and they even have names

What's on the menu, what can I eat?
My McDonalds has shut, it's only down the High Street

Heinz you ONLY made 57 in variety
That won't last long in a locked down society

I watched Columbo when flares were in fashion
Why must my bacon sarnie suffer because of the ration?

Will I have to talk to the family and be nice to the wife?
But we walked down the aisle in love and she's the best part of my life

I could read a book, get myself educated
Try a little yoga, meditate, not be agitated

Go running, as allowed, once a day
Reduce my waist size, go all the way

Plant some seeds, watch them grow
Learn new things which I didn't know

Support my family, stay focused and strong
I can survive this, no matter how long

Search your soul, inside is a fighter
On the other side it's warmer and lighter

Look in the mirror, look at your face
You can do this, you're the brilliant unstoppable, fantastic human race

John's Gone …
Granville Daniel Clarke

He went in his sleep last night. It was time to go.

The cheer up smiles from visitors were becoming weary.
Waxwork-tears finished ages ago and everybody knew.

Crabs are very nice in the pub, over a pint,
Or with a mixed salad at home,
But not when the little sods are eating your neck.

The great technological scientific wizards are still
Struggling for the magic potion for this one.
And John goes.

Bring on the screens nurse...
Wobbly castors rumble over an old wood floor,
sounding and echoing like a hallowed death knell.
Through the faded screen curtains gloomy lights
cast a collage of fast moving shadows,
leap around in the enclosed space,
and project upwards onto the ceiling above,
displaying themselves shadow puppet fashion,
involved in some bizarre ghostly dance …
after the ball was over …

The patiently resident bedtime orchestra tunes in.
The Oblivious Flatulent Snoring Blanket Bugles Band
are playing a moonlight saunter,
accompanied tonight by the
Swishing Swashing Disinfectant Wafters Dance Team
trying to compete with death's strange unique odour.
More hurried footsteps creep …
shorter … tighter … tenser …
whispered voice work … hushed …
clearly, closely together … strain
of lifting …
in unison … precise …
Done.

continued overleaf …

Illustration © Granville D Clarke

Not much weight on him, a lightweight burden ... the
wobbly wheels start to roll behind the screen ... the
screen wheels move adjacent, in perfect harmony with the internal trolley ... a
clever exercise in the art of
obliteration, using two moveable objects.

A macabre piece of conjured magic, that didn't wait for any applause -
the bedband were still oblivious, whilst still playing their trumpets, and I was the
only audience ...
The show is over.

As the rumbling wheels fade away down the Hospital corridor
taking another predictable passenger on his last ride ...
not much of a glory trail
not very heavenly at all
not a saint in sight
no angelic choir
no aerial cameras panning out,
wide and skyward ... with rising orchestral volume and swell ...
just a squeaking trolley
and three gingham clad night nurses ...

Or was I looking the wrong way ... ? ...

3.30 am. New Year's Day 1980 Brentwood Hospital, Essex.

Days and Trials of Fibrillation
Granville Daniel Clarke

Early sunlight shadows stream across a tired wrinkled curtain
As another day dawns to shine on as a Hospital ward's docile
occupants slowly arouse, to the Morning shift nursing staff's arrival
to wake and cajole.

Cheery dispositions abound as
Fresh water jugs dispensed
Foul urine jugs disposed
Tablets and tea, breakfast, all free.

My heart still races, intent on continued fibrillation
as the daily machine informs
through my many attached body wires acquired to check and
control … hundred and fifty … coming down …
twenty thirty … back to sixty …
heart-rate still high … conformed to lie …
To be a patient patient.

More days to face being married to my monitor
Still wired, still tired
as the blood pump high heart rate endangered my being
to stroke or attack.
So now, embraced in a caring system,
Guarded by technology and humanity
Living the trials of heartfelt fibrillation.

This Generation
Sophie Ryall

They baked a revolution in secret
Through their telephones and screens
Stroked the fires of rebellion
Determined to expel racism and its creed

By the stove they whispered
From Hertfordshire to Tower Hamlet

Boris was worried about knife crime
Talked about county lines,
Gang violence, cited Grime
As the source of dissatisfaction and disarray

He ignored the barriers placed on us
Trapped and entangled us
Forgot the laws that targeted us, from our hair regulations to tags on our
ankles,
Feeding the criminal systems meant
To ~~protect~~
Profit
Off us.

He complained about radicalization
The segregation
of our communities, the failure to integrate
When really they feared our ability to
Elevate

White rage, its cloak covering their privilege
A blanket washing the world and its struggles,
Artificial hurt, dismissal, attempting to hold the divide

Acrid smoke fills our noses
Anger explosive, the racism corrosive
Eating away at each generation,
Head down, Survive.

They clapped for us
Rainbows sparkling in the shade

but for the past two years there has been nothing but hate.
Brexit days, alt-right rallies, blame and complaints

And now the Storm is breaking
Thunder shaking
Earth shattering, impacting
Anger like lightning burning in our veins
People flood the streets, like warm rain after a summer's day
voices chanting high, shared pain

Red paint splashed on shining metal skin
Blood of long forgotten sins
Whitewashed into a revered hero

Edward Colson
Slaver, Educator,
Cold water, engulfs, submerges,
Sinking to the blackness of the depths

The ugly truth already pollutes the river
Hundreds of bound screams
Slap against the wall like waves
Tied hands, now inherited from slaves to the trader

My mother's tears fall on lined printed-paper
A gag order
silenced after she explained how
they hurt her

Another Black man died on his hands and feet
Whole communities grieve
Already brought to their knees

Crippled by centuries of exploitation, segregation
Gentrification,
Greed

Weighing down on our chests,
George Floyd's last words

"I Can't
Breathe"

Trapped
Sophie Ryall

And I sit on my bed, walls an ivory tower
Flowers that entrap, encircle
Purple hyacinth winking by the door

Vines like tendrils wrap around my throat, choking
The silence from it

Buoyed by the voices of a thousand others
The blacker the berry,
The sweeter the juice

Corona fills our TV, our houses
Lulling us into a false sense of equality
But ultimately the piles of bodies at the bottom
Of the inquiry
are not
White

Covid's shadow stalks our streets
But the darkness Britain hides
has been with us for far longer

Isolation sinks its barbs into your skin, cutting into
the flesh
That feeds the nation
Empty farms, empty
Wide eyes, soft brown skin
little fingers held in detention centres.

The feeling of trapped-ness, tendrils holding you in
place
Weighing further on the shackles of oppression
Having to pick between survival today or a broken
tomorrow

Both options taste like death
One is just slower
Crippled by decades of institutionalized
oppression, discrimination
No legal representation
Our communities now facing gentrification
Brixton's stalls shutting, Streatham centre stops
pounding

Raw emotion ignites; billions across the world
unite,
Blood slashes on the street, whispers of revolution
are held tight
Rubber bullets pound like drum beats,
Matching my frantic heartbeat, protest sign lifted
high
Screams rise out, tearing apart the night

The voices of freedom float up
Echoing from shore to shore
Chanting

Black
Lives
Matter

Illustration: 'Beneath the Veil' © Anne Genner Crawford

Ci Manchi Nonno[1].
Isabelle Lepore

It was on Easter Sunday,
halfway through fitting
a pastry case into a steel-scalloped tray
That we heard you'd gone.

We stood numb
Pacing from kitchen floor to front door,
Faces made raw
with mourning and thumbed-through flour.

The day was bright, and though
Light and heat exasperated,
evaporated tears,
they fell silently within.

By noon, calls had already been made
And the crust was golden by then.
For a moment, I thought on the rim
of the pie as a halo.

Over the Easter meal our thoughts
Of you with glass, in hand,
glinting and raised to toast the family tidings.
Wine red, cheeks tired from laughing,
now from bearing the heavy-lidded
weight of loss.

Intonations raised,
our hopeful voices
clamoured for your recovery,
that the strength of fear and love would revive
and give you healthy
release from infections gyves.

He sang the day before he died.
Those Tarantella tunes,
pulsed in his thickly-set wrists;
they will play on and on.

Images: wallpaperflare

And the eye mists
with quick, trickling tears that are gone
In furious, instant swoons
When remembering

I cannot see him shuffle
Steadfastly to the garden.
Again, to the shed, laden with the ruffle
Heads of cabbage, hardened
and dried by the sun,
to feed pecking hens.

Plodding back with Figs fresh,
Pea-pods plump,
A summer feast of fruit flesh
we'd eat together beside the mesh
of Chicken wire.

How we wanted to embrace
On the day.
To talk the grief away,
over Mulino Bianco biscuits
From the battered tin with teas,
Vanilla soft when soaked in milk
or dunked in sweet coffee memories.

Nonna[2] looks for you in the house,
You are not there;
Seeing your empty chair
Stagnant, bereft, bare,
I feel only now how you were a pair.

To hear her howls the soul did jolt,
harpooned by searing cries, disparate
from strained labour or the bolt
Of revulsion from salted wounds.
She was torn, irreparably torn.
Eyes, shrunken from sorrow,
Tissues torn, reused,
soaking up loose droplets

That would otherwise water
the seasoned ground,
where all of our eyes were lowered.
Where spade and fork were laid
To make way for you, for

the low-rising mane of chrysanthemums
that still Weep with light at your going,
and crown the head of your turf-bed.
Knowing, as the pall bearers lead,
the moment came to lay you to rest.

Gesù lo ricorda quando
viene nel tuo regno;
Dov'è il passato? Molto tempo fa… non lo so.
Ci Manchi Nonno. Come la croce di legno

di Christo,[3]
you were placed to rest,
in wood then into the chalk,
white like bone, of the earth.
You were not taken by time,
to me. For I could not be there
To hold, to sit beside.
Invisible,
on the day of resurrection

Still, I will say Ciao[4] Nonno,
Every time, I stand by your grave.
Ciao Nonno,
A greeting blessed, as
I know that
You hear me still.

1   *Grandfather*
2   *Grandmother*
3   *Jesus, remember Him, when*
      He comes into your kingdom.
      Where is the past? Long ago… I don't know.
      We miss you Grandad. Like the wooden cross of Christ.
4   *Goodbye, but also the informal Hello*

127

She is my fighter pilot
Joe Solo

She is my fighter pilot.
Her Spitfire an old Renault 5;
She isn't shooting the enemy down,
She's keeping people alive.

She is my fighter pilot.
Putting her life on the line,
In this new hidden Battle of Britain,
She answers the call every time.

She is my fighter pilot.
Her medal a round of applause;
From the doorsteps of this grateful nation;
While she gives her life to the cause.

She is my fighter pilot.
We're all of us now in her debt.
And when this new war is over,
We must never, never forget.

Illustration © Alan Andrews

This is our Blitz
Joe Solo

This is our Blitz.
No sound of bombs, nor siren's drone;
Our deaths will hide away at home;
This war's behind closed doors,
It's me and mine, it's you and yours;
Self-isolated in our shelters,
Playing the hand that fate has dealt us;
Who knows where the next bomb hits?
This is our Blitz.
This is our Blitz.
And like before, we'll face the worst:
The poverty, that always cursed
Us puts us now on the front line,
Where some will buckle, some will shine,
Yet most will sail this sea of trouble,
And rise up once more from the rubble,
Hands held out though hearts in bits.
This is our Blitz.

Illustration © Alan Andrews

Listen for a Tweet
Amber Hawkins

Headphones on so we don't hear the birds sing
Silent mode off so we can hear the phone ring
People all around but no-one to speak to
No idea if they'll treat you or cheat you
The world can't breathe, the world can't breathe
If you keep on this way, you'll be forced to grieve

So many texts, no real conversations
A world full of beings yet such split nations
It is the people's globe, the greatest race
Yet with endless creatures, planets and Space
Can this really be the case?
The world can't breathe, we need to leave
It needs to heal, and we need to grieve

A man's world, but a virus locks us in
A man's world, well maybe it might have been
But with greed and arrogance, we lost touch with the others
We are all animals, mothers are mothers
The world will heal, and the world will breathe
We will thrive soon, but first we grieve

Stay inside, be thankful for security
Cherish each moment, grow in maturity
Focus on relationships, take nothing for granted
And despite our old perceptions being slanted
We will love our Earth and love each other
Treat all the same, for a mother is a mother
So while we grieve for the lost, and grieve for the past
We will learn to live so that we can last
The world is healing, and the world is breathing
From now on please let's listen to the birds sing.

Illustration © Howard Aynhoe

Isolation
Edsard Driessen

I sit on the edge of the world and wait.
Wait until skylight returns and the flooding fields in front of me
march the beaches to my left.
I wait until the golden sun turns to amber, where the night sky
Invades the marshes.
I wait until gloves are removed, and it is illegal again to walk into a
bank with a masked face.
I wait until waiting in waiting lines is no longer denoted by duct tape
on concrete,
Where strangers are treated with kindness, not suspicion, where a
smoker's cough is just a smoker's cough.
Where our freedom returns, the conflict ceases, till the guns sound no
more
We wave our white flag.
Till the shadows stay absent no longer,
The fluorescent clouds leave my brain.
Always existing on the horizon line, till the sun catches me unarmed
no more.
Illuminate my paused state of existence and cast hopes and dreams to
another timeline
Till you've seen me
Raw and bare.
Clutching onto false optimism like the elderly to walking aids.
Welcome the sunset and the eclipse,
Where we wait,
Perpetually suspended in grip.

Locked Down Pigeon
Rachel Feldberg

For the last four weeks
The wood pigeon and I
Have been watching each other.
She on her nest, me on my chair
And then, yesterday
She left – without a word.

I can understand her feelings
Sitting like that
With nothing to do,
Locked down on her bundle of twigs.

I'd been worrying
About her mental health.
Whether she had enough stimulation
With only occasional visits
From her mate, taking his turn
So she could walk cautiously
Round the garden
Eyeing my sister's seedlings.

It's not as if
We hadn't been communicating,
I talked to her every day
Telling her what I'd been up to.
But she left, just like that.
I suppose she'd had it with waiting.

Now the sparrows have come
And are taking her nest apart.

Illustration © Bryan Ledgard

Bearing Fruit
Ellen Waters

Today, the tree in our garden
started bearing fruit. Usually, this marks
the start of a glorious period of
sticky purple fingers, edging carefully
around the stiff, solid centre,
gathering plums in smeary Tupperware –
and then, when they are all full, in saucepans,
coffee mugs, raspberry punnets,
old butter pots, outstretched palms,
the smooth scoop of my skirt,
anything we have to hand that can
reign in this sweet, expanding mass of
English summer. Then we will
stand back to marvel at our
temporary treasure before shipping it out –
four tubs to each friend and foe,
three on the doorstep of an elderly neighbour,
two to the postman,
one an honorary guest
to every dinner party and barbecue.
Twenty thousand steps, giving out that
which we cannot hope to finish on our own.
Now, the postman tosses
our letters over the fence.
The streets run dry.
I worry what we will do
with all this ephemeral harvest.

Today, I see the tree in
our garden start to bear fruit
and I stand back,
and I wonder what is
the point of growth
if I suddenly have no one
to share it with.

Illustration © Charley Wright

Last Night
Ellen Waters

You lean across acres of stiff
white sheets to plant a kiss
on my forehead. Your lips,
paper-thin and tinged
with pink like the horizon edges
of your brain, rest on my skin
just long enough to show me
everything your mouth never had
time to form. For a second, you are
the only language my tongue can still
wrap itself around. Somewhere between
our interlocked souls, a sliver of eternity
is trapped. Just before you pull away,
I feel the swansong of your pulse
drumming against colourless cheeks

and I know this is the final piece of you
I want to remember.

Illustration: 'Lost Kiss' © Charley Wright

Spring Cleaning
Ellen Waters

That morning, gold leaks into
her window and pours like silk
across her aching eyelids. From muggy black,
she wakes and basks in the caress of
a fresh day, steps out into an age of
glint and green and throws the white sheets
of her arms towards the heavens.

That morning, she paints her darkness in
vivid colours across the sky, watches smoke
seep from chapped lips and swirl into mist,
banished to another subconscious;
it couldn't belong to her, not that morning.
That morning, her lungs proclaim to the open moors
and dare them to fill her with anything but air.

That morning, she tips seeds into the
yearning soil and breathes in crystal emptiness,
thanking this new world for all it has
given her and all it has taken away.

Illustration © Paul Almond

Vow
Ellen Waters

On a sunny day, all those years ago,
they went South for the weekend to

watch the sun swing across the amber
sky and the waves stroke the shoreline

with all the tenderness of a lover's touch.
New love burning in the pits of their

stomachs, they laced their fingers together
and marvelled at a single lark streaking

into song before them, struck by the
simple majesty of this tiny thing and its

wild, vibrant refrain. Years later, she would
tell me it was the last time she ever saw

a lark. Their homes left and they followed,
leaving only a whisper in the air and their

notes, captured in the ascending hum
of violin strings in flight.

She didn't know it then; she didn't
know so much. Perhaps if they had looked

deep enough into each other's eyes, they
would have seen it all: the ring that she

still wears around her finger like a psalm;
a family with love enough to fill the

whole country as it grew; a half left behind.
But it couldn't have mattered, not that day.

They were young, the tide was high
and the world smouldered with promise.

Illustration © Becky McMurray

Ghost Light
Ellen Waters

He is locking up for the last time.
The air, normally heaving with talk and sweat
and tightly-packed bodies yearning for
something to thrill them,
sings itself to sleep
if only to cover the hole it cannot
stretch to fill.
This is his haven, his battleground, and
he does not know when he will get to
see it again.
This has been heaven for him,
and hell.

He takes a minute to scan around once again
before bolting the door behind him.
The wings still trembling with the residue
of anxious chatter and last-minute chaos;
each seat still indented with the memory
of its last occupant cradled into fabric;
the walls creaking with the weight of lines
and stories left suddenly unspoken;

and, taking centre stage, the ghost light,
casting its silent beams in the promise
that one day soon, it will take its final bow,
and the applause will return.

Illustration © Becky McMurray

Certificate
Aidan Quigley

Closer than life
    at times,

with a border only
millimetres thin
to keep me from the
other side of this skin,

But still so far,
    somehow …

Always an 'is'
or a 'will',
    never a *been* …

Always some other actor's scene
To play out with the waxy sheen
And painted eyes of sleep.

It's nothing to be known,
for sure,
Never alive, but grown
early in the heart, like
Shrapnel; buried deep
Yet apart, unconcerned with all this *us*-ness…

For as hard as I try, I know

That skin, in a tailored suit
that doesn't fit him,
That isn't *it*…

Isn't him, either … It's just …
    not …

It seems surprised with itself
to find its vision tangled, only
seeing once it's all unravelled the *nots*
that were there all along,

tied up in us, held fast
and gordian in the tendons;
threads to be cut,
not solved or undone,

just

Resolved,
like everything else these days,

with the dull lift of defeat
and no tears under ken
of eyes too ashamed to open.

Extenuating Circumstances
Aidan Quigley

so. ends don't seem like ends it seems.
no bang. not even a whimper.
just a fraying out of somethings into nothings
until it all sits within a whisper;
a few words that trickle down the breeze
in drops, like hemlock down a string …

                while somewhere
dressed in sun and green
fruit grows fat and ripe on trees,
as the dolphins swim closer to shore
now the water's clear of all this
muddied emotion …

for emotion has to move to be itself
– that I know – to keep moving and moving 'til
moving just mirrors stillness' steps.
       I know
all that, and yet,
even though I'm different
from each thought to the next,
I find that living's still no move at all;

just a *'going through the motions …'*

Baptism
Aidan Quigley

There was a rankling light
that gnawed through the
fissures in the Giant's
fingers, and there was

a tenderness of terror
in the trembling of hands
that reached into the sink
to bathe the child

like a dog in the kitchen;
to brush away the dust
off this fresh fossil
and mine this clay of

their own for meaning.
It seems easy now to drape
a wholeness of nothing
over what's barely the

skeleton of a memory,
flayed of all the flesh
of language, stripped
of every sibilant morsel,

each plosive plucked bare
by the crows. But somewhere
In the sun spilling over the cusp,
In the porcelain freckled with suds,

In those same, ice-bright eyes
That find the heat to thaw at last,
In the curve of the moment,
There was still that something

That stood like fear,
but led like love for all its
lumbering.

Illustration: 'Legacy Variation' © John A McPake

This Be the Monumental Verse …

(from the statue of Larkin in Hull's Paragon Station.)
Brian W. Lavery

They cover for me, the literary classes.
They won't admit it, but they do. And all at
Pains not to reveal what I really thought of you:
Working crass, reds, wimmin and children of migration
Who all pass me daily while minding their station.

Motion-less misanthrope
In this city of poets I
Stare down the line in
Stone cold fury at casting
Of pearl before swine.

No Marvell hero I – but on a Paragon's pedestal for coming years
While my cold metal façade hides my deepest fears.
That while stuck – unable to move an inch – the children of
The future will know me better then – and rip me from my plinth.

Occasional comfort in my dread – while I stand forever still – is
That I know they will always love me at the old Hull Lit. and Phil..

Illustration © Tony Heald

Times and Tides
Brian W. Lavery

Maternal fathers strong to save
– mam and dad to lad and lass
And men who took the
harvest from the waves.

Terrace ender tell-tale talk from
women who never waved…
Nor wavered … but buried secret fears
where they also hid their tears.

Constant fight to feed the bains
Tank-like prams booled by mams
Racing for absent men's wages –
A dock of aegis, cleft for thee.

Scruffy kids frozen in
Perpetual Play Street gaze
Waiting for Dad's kitbag,
– Christmas every twenty-one days.

Ever-watching Gert and Lil
lean from terrace window sill
You be-have-ing you, Bill or
I tell yer mam … I will.

Three tides later – a latch-key
Lifted in click so-quietly – so
The two-up fretting wife won't
Wave her man away.

Grey-silhouetted deckie in the
Humber haar drops his
gear in a Subway Car to
catch the company store.

And cathedral wireless crackling
mimics bacon sizzle and
departures in morning's half-light

'… Dogger, Fisher, German Bight …'

Illustration © Tony Heald

Neighbourhood Watch
Rosemary Evans

piano-playing from number 47
the steady trickle of quavers through the wall
and number 12 with the television always on
flashing game-show pink through the curtains

and the segments on the news
with families tumbling over each other
messy attempts at home-schooling
painting rainbows on the windows
noisy stories of this and her and he
skype calls and zoom calls
grinning through webcams
waving from doorsteps
squabbles and tears no doubt
but splashes of joy in the corners
making the best of it

but no word yet on
the houses without pianos
or televisions
the houses doused in silence

all the stories that are not at this moment being told
were never being told in the first place.

Illustration © Bryan Ledgard

When The Dog Bites The Monkey
Heath Common

When the dog bites the monkey
You gotta wonder what's gonna happen next
See, the dog's normally so placid
It's the most obedient of all the pets
But the monkey's always gotta push it
Just to see how far he can go

(well the damned thing's gone too far now, so he's gotta go!)

And when the dog bites the hand that feeds him
And the blood begins to flow
And the dog holds on to the hand in his mouth
When normally he'd be inclined to let go
You gotta wonder 'is this the end of the beginning?'
Or is this the start of something else?'

(I don't know but I'm worried just the same)

Now I'm not suggesting revolution
And I'm not suggesting fighting in the streets
(I don't know but whoever does know about these things?)
But I ask you just how much more teasing can that poor, damned dog take?
Before he snaps and he howls and he finally stands up for himself and he declares :

In the spirit of the people, this dog's not gonna take it anymore
Now I'm normally well behaved and I usually accept everything you say
But you keep pushing and pulling and snapping at my tail and winding me up each and every day and …
Oh dammit!

No more of your dodgy expenses claims!
No more of your rigged inspections!
No more of your stupid 'judgements'!
No more of your compulsory redundancies!
'Cos as Sonny Boy Williamson once said
"Don't start me talking
'Cos I'll tell everything I know!"

Now talk some sense man and do the right thing!

Illustration © Terry Brookes

Nightingale Street
Sophie Lutkin

It was *Sleeping Beauty* tonight at number one.
Maleficent had just begun
her infamous curse, when behind the door,
a wearied pair of eyes she saw.
As if by magic, the horns disappeared;
the cloak unfurled, the scowl cleared,
and in their place a mother stood,
book in hand – she understood
her husband's look, the knitted brow,
the exhausted hope she'd seen just now.
Smoothing the sleeves of his scrubs,
she holds him close; he goes to rub
the tousled hair of his son, his daughter.
A different kind of tired. Her eyes water.
He kisses them all, a soft *Goodnight* –
was this the last time he would turn off the light?

It was laundry at number three
when the scent of sandalwood carried her overseas,
back to China, to her father, her mother,
to the smile on the face of her little brother.
She had read the time apart through her changes in attire,
from the duffel coat to the shorts worn at last year's bonfire,
and now the scarf of the grandmother that had passed –
a season of sadness she hoped would not last.
She breathed in her country, looked out at the rain,
but knew, in her heart, she would see them again.

It was chaos at number six
as he tried to work out how to mix
the birthday cake batter with a defiant appliance,
at the same time as teaching his son about science.
Butter, flour, sugar – he was sure there was something more …
Eggs are an emulsifier, his son read, as he picked the mixture off the floor.
When his husband blew out the candles at the end of the day,
the lesson that was learnt was love always finds a way.

continued overleaf …

Illustration © Becky McMurray

It was an anxious wait at number eight,
pacing the floor, wondering why she was late.
The air was thick, she couldn't bear to look –
she fiddled with her shirt, picked up and put down a book.
And then those two blue lines, like margins on a page,
appeared in her hands, lit her living room like a stage.
Everywhere was silver, a warm glow like pearls,
as she wondered whether it would be a boy or a girl.

It was tea and cake at number eleven
as he looked lovingly at the wife who'd had a near brush with heaven.
Sixty-five years, three great-grandchildren, and a World War together;
he thought he had lost her, but every storm they would weather.
Time just as precious now as it was when they were young,
no waltz they wouldn't dance to, no song left unsung.
He read the lines of those hands that had taken him as his wife,
the wrinkles on the face that had smiled her way through life,
the royal blue earrings pinned proudly in her ear,
and thanked all the nurses that meant she was here.

It was just before sunrise at number twelve,
and a mother was busying herself over pan and shelve.
There was comfort in knowing that this food they could share,
reading the Quran, as they rose for morning prayer.

It was a momentous day at number fifteen,
with gown and mortarboard, he listened to the dean
read off his name from his back-garden porch,
a doctor prematurely, to carry forward that brave torch.

Back home again at number one,
the birds were singing, the day had begun,
when a warrior quietly returned home from war,
took off his shoes, closed his front door.
He needed to hold his children, his wife;
needed to know they were safe, needed to hold onto *life*.
Climbing the staircase, he kisses the hair
of his young children, lying in sweet sleep there.
A fairy-tale prince, fighting the dragons unending,
determined that this story would have a happy ending.

Vulcan's Flame
Sophie Lutkin

Let us not with the courage in our minds
Admit apprehension. Strength is not strength
Which falters when it alteration finds,
Or just once challenged, disappears at length.
O no! it is an ever-burning glow
That lights from within and does never tremble;
It is the source of every river's flow,
Whose spirit known, would Neptune resemble.
Strength's not Time's fool, though doubt and unease tries
Within to cabin, crib, confine again;
Strength falters not with the candle's demise
But whose wax lives on by the sculptor's pen.
If this be error and upon me proved,
Let my ink dry and the stars stand, unmoved.

Dad's Ladders
Lynda Rose Morgan

I have dad's ladders now.
Though they are not used much
they are indispensable.
Anytime I like I can run
a finger over the past.
I can feel the Braille characters of a knobbly
moment when the paint splashed
a step.
Memories of rooms we painted
together are condensed
into elegant white gloss pennies
strewn on the footholds.
Fingerprints of frosted lilacs
flower over the handrail.
My mistake the red
a lonely puddle
on the top tread.
Today I slip my foot into yours
as I ascend the ladder,
to add another memory.
Terracotta and green.
The colour of my new kitchen.

Illustration © Bryan Ledgard

Gratitude
Rozana Ahmad Huq

In the dark of the night
I dig deep into my heart,
Searching for an answer, a light.

How shall I wrap this precious gift of life?

With a shiny paper of gold
Or something plain and brown and not so bold?
With pink and blue ribbons?
Diamond, sapphire and emerald sequins?

How shall I wrap this precious gift?

I look through the window
Rain splattering against the glass,
Staring at me with their big eyes
Droplets of tears run down my cheeks.

I question myself again,
and again…

How shall I wrap this precious gift of joy and happiness?

Tiny hands, a strong grip
Signalling a bond,
Loveable smile
Sparkling eyes looking into mine,
Soft breath
The smell of creation.

Suddenly,
A stream of light,
It was dawn
I had not realised.

Birth of a new day
I enter the light
Butterfly breaks loose
The answer crystallizes.

It doesn't need to be
A shiny paper, an emerald or sapphire,
Not even a diamond stone.

I shall wrap it with the
Gem of Gratitude.

Born in Florence
Rozana Ahmad Huq

Rebelling against the
Stereotype role of upper-class women
The expectations to be a mother and wife
She broke the rule.

Followed her instinct, her spiritual 'call'
This she wrote in her diary during her travels
To Thebes and Egypt
And in her letter to her sister, Parthenope.

Battling against diseases of malaria, cholera
In her pursuit of caring for the sick
She fought tooth and nail to bring about
Laws of sanitization and hygiene in medicine and nursing.

Horrified by the dead and the wounded
In the Crimean war
Her compassion, commitment and dedication
Grew stronger.
And, in the darkness of the night, when she wafted through the wards
Drug-drowsed survivors wondered
"Am I awake or asleep?"
The descent of an Angel who carried her lamp
"A vision? A dream that I wake but I keep?"
As they whispered their ode to their Nightingale.

Illustration © Bryan Ledgard

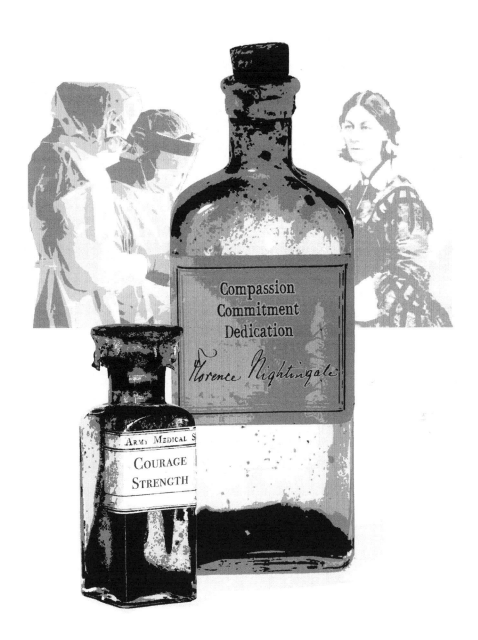

The Seven Stages of Ignorant Grief
Nes Vanriel-Edwards

What is happening?
Is everybody poisoned?
Am I infected?

BoJo's on the news
I don't know much, nor does he
Where's his right hand man?

I need to get food
There's no pasta in the shops
They won't deliver…

Woo, I'm off work now
Pasta is back on the shelves
Might get used to this.

Tick Tock, bored o'clock
Starting to get a bit much
Might break the rules now

Heard a friend's nan died
Feeling nervous once again
Best to stay indoors …

Stay inside please, mate
Make sure you cover your face
If you go outside.

Beached
Louise Larkinson

I bathe your fevered flesh, prop you up on
a shore of Egyptian cotton. Your corona eyes
track my every move.
Sorry I couldn't keep you safe, we were mismatched
from the start. Me a lion – you a fish.

I offer potato mash; fork *I love you*
in its creamy topping. You fork back
three wobbly *XXX.*
Spurred on, I muster my lion strength
enfold you in my arms and lift.

We make it to the window. You
breathe hard – misting the glass;
look, you cry *I'm not finished yet.*
Hope takes flight from Pandora's Box.
Perhaps we will get down to the sea tomorrow.

Shedding
Pamela Leadbetter

I keep my distance to stop you
Shedding over me
Something so terrifying
it will invade my lungs in a strangulated grip of sharpened steel
Robbing me of speech, thought and the comfort of loved ones
But what I find right now is
Oh for sure you are shedding over me
This
Layer after layer of thoughtful kindness
A treat I've missed from the shops but could not get
Waving away it took four shops to find a queue not a barricade
A Sunday roast dinner cooked with your customary skill and left on my doorstep
garnished with love
A shared smile over the Clapping
A sense of being held in community and belonging
Zooming into your dear familiar face and laughter
We are shedding our stiff upper layers swaying together in the lockdown dance
Bridges vanquishing metres

Scale
Alice Manning

If I were to enlarge the farce that is
the effect of the growing proportions of this virus –
this monstrosity, not only for its lives-rampage,
but the scores and scores of souls left
without an outlet. Without. Let it
not detract from the life that is lost. But impress the need
to visualize in pre-styled text the reality
of the millions. Work, school, social (life) –
bars and cafés, colleges and churches,
beaches and ballrooms, football fields and florists –
all shut. All gone. Whether it was
semblance of reality sought in consumerism,
or the life-blood of our daring human dreams,
we ran on it; our little freedoms in this limited life.
The scale of that cannot be denied.

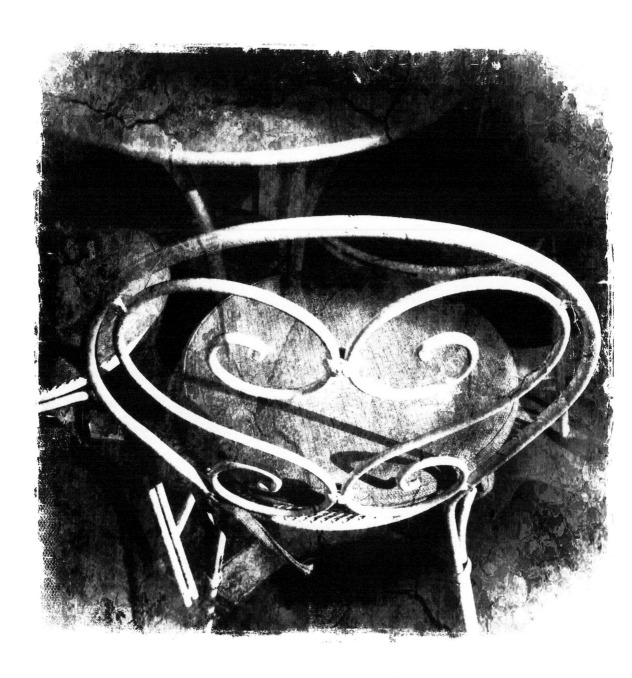

Together, But Apart
Alice Manning

But apart suggests we are
a part of this –
this oxymoronic word/phrase
suited to our sorry state –
this whole bloody thing,
expelled across streets and offices,
saturating cities and sleepy villages,
sweeping the carpets and painting the walls,
as you bear witness to where
you sat with friends on a Saturday evening,
mid-afternoon, a Monday morning,
an anyday anything.
Now – the same chair, same table –
remembering, forgetting what the old ordinary felt like.

Illustration © Mel Ledgard

Viral/virtual/virus
Alice Manning

They'll look back and say:
'We kept in touch. All in the same boat.'
Or *s*. Plural. Little lifeboats, moored away from freedom;
Crushed in, aerodynamic sardines.

The real and the virtual: virtual = almost there.
I'm there, virtually. I'm riding a wave
To where I don't know,
But you're in it, pretending that you're not.

My thoughts circulate like virus droplets.

'When routine bites hard
And ambitions are low', think:
Virtual happy hour! Drinks at a distance!
Viral has gone viral.

I'm (virtually) with you. I'm the Dire Straits,
Singing 'so far away from me'.
You're there in the distance and how I feel for you
Has *become* viral; the very cells

I can no longer control, aghast at me.

Illustration © Mel Ledgard

Love in Lockdown
Gareth Griffith

Shall I compare thee to a summer's day?
 I can't – I'm not allowed to go outside
And, when I did, you stood six feet away
 In facemask and lots of bactericide,
And so I've no idea if you're like summer,
 Or what you're like at all, or (truth be told)
What summer days are like. It's quite a bummer.
 No wonder that my passion's growing cold.
But several times a day, for twenty seconds,
 I sing you 'Happy Birthday' like a dope,
Because that's long enough (the doctor reckons)
 To beat coronavirus. We can hope.
        So social distancing has not yet quashed
        The love recalled each time my hands are washed.

Illustration © Terry Brookes

The Ruins at Babylon
Matthew Walker

Caught between two moments,
I find myself imagining
the high walls of Babylon.

Though the seconds continue past me,
I am held there,
enraptured,
by the feel of the moving air,
and the sight of Quinces against the brush.

Far off in the distance, I can hear
the perfectly even,
unreal
ticking of the clock.
Each of its movements
take me by the throat
and I close my eyes as I try to breathe.

Again, I am in Babylon,
as a funeral procession
passes through the gates.

I am told it is Alexander.

Perhaps he too
felt the weight of time
bearing down.

All that is left of Babylon is ruins.

Illustration © Sophie Ioakim

91 Farm Road
Violet Hatch

At 91 Farm Road there is a lady on 'lockdown',
She's missing getting on the bus and going into town.
She fills her time with baking, but it's hard to keep it merry,
When you're nearly out of flour, with one last glacé cherry.

At 91 Farm Road there is a lady who will knit,
(We don't know where those blankets go to, come to think of it?)
She sometimes hears the doorbell ring,
But when she gets up from the chair,
She finds a lonely bag of food but no-one else is there.

At 91 Farm Road, the lady likes to get a call,
Most often from 2 daughters (well, you cannot win them all).
Margaret at eight thirty, and Nicola at four
Caroline 'tween six and seven,
And Sylvia (the bore!)

At 91 Farm Road a lady reads *The Peoples Friend*
It's not very well written
But she still would recommend.
A cup of tea with oatcakes
Ample enough and never stale,
Then settles for the evening with the chatty Ian Dale.

At 91 Farm Road, it's a lockdown like no other
You may know lovely Mrs Giles,
I know her as 'grandmother'.
And when we're free to roam again
And when she's eighty-eight
We'll all be there at 91, at 91's back gate.

Illustration © Stephanie McRobert

Evenings in Isolation
Violet Hatch

We've exhausted the banana bread,
Mum's scared she might have flu,
Making tea and baking mad,
Even the oven's tired too.
All books of every genre read,
The kettles been abused,
Dog walks are far more frequent,
And the dog is not amused.
New ventures and old hobbies,
Same house but different space,
Poor postman with our packages
Trudging from place to place.
Won't stray beyond the portico
Far from the wooden gate,
I say farewell to Spring this year,
I'll sit aside and wait.
Seeing photographs of schedules,
Old videos of smiles,
As I while away my hours,
With some long and lonely whiles.
Tick tock the clocks are out of sync
Piano notes play out of tune
With birds that chirrup songs of Spring
As twilight's sun brings summer's moon.

The Visitor
Violet Hatch

Outside the visitor has landed
Something hanging in the air,
Spitting, coughing, dirty handed,
Throat, then lungs, intensive care.

The lane now busier than the town,
Observe our social distance.
The businesses have all closed down
In the fight to gain resistance.

Saved for tomorrow each tiny task
Is savoured and drawn out.
Behind the nurse's sweaty mask
A frown of fear and doubt.

And in the sunny empty park,
A barbecue creates a spark,
Run, cycle, walk for activity
And talk- but not so close to me.

The workers receive weekly applause
As bodies queue in hospital morgues
And Boris fights to save the day
Not ventilated yet they say.

But in the post, there's seeds to sow
We live in hope today,
Outside the visitor has landed,
How long before they go away?

Ode to Gerald
Elizabeth Brown

Right, so, there's this pigeon.
(I have named him Gerald)
He's a regular this spring,
Visible from my humble bed.
Due to the 'current situation',
I'm sure this is a popular sitting spot for all –
Of course, they don't have Gerald for company.
(Neither do they know this secret)
The secret is, my dear Gerald,

I have been here before the spring
And I will be here after;
And it's not me alone, but many.
The secret is our isolation is different;
Different because it's not for the pandemic;
Different because it's not optional,
It definitely won't end before August,
No matter what the chaps in London say.

Enjoy your little escapes! (remember you are lucky)
Daily walks aren't really our thing,
But it's nice to watch people through the window
(No one is as lovely as my Gerald though)

Maybe Gerald is like me!
The tree is his sitting spot,
His condition is chronic (iconic),
His boredom contained;
He could always tell our secret –
That would be nice of him.

I do hope Gerald stays the year.

Illustration © Bryan Ledgard

So Long
Hannah Ludlow

It's been a week since we said so long.
Hope still reigns, no aches and pains yet
Fill the heart.
But like a mountain seems small
From a distance,
Little did we know that
Our love would become our yellow streak,
And this week would turn into weeks and weeks
Until that last goodbye became a
Distant memory.

It's been a month since we said so long.
'I miss you' we express
To a screen – I see your face
But long for an embrace,
A wealth of memories stolen
Before they were even made.
Our youth ticks on and like a time bomb
We feel the pressure to live our young lives to the full.
But for now we wait, slow down and love
From a distance.

It's been some time since we said so long.
Summer arrives, and with it a sense that we must
Rise with the sun, relinquish the pressure that weighs a tonne
And appreciate that through the tough times
On this rough road we two are one.
But soon this heat becomes a toxic fume
That fills our lungs with grief and our minds with
Anger. Anger at the hours wrenched from us,
This vicissitude imposed on us,
And the distance forced between us.

It's been so long since we said so long.
A measuring tape now separates
Me from your lips, which used to decorate
My walls, floors, ceilings and doors.
Every centimetre mocks that love we took for granted,
Those seeds we planted – our love still grows
But its direction is different. Distance endures
Us and we endure distance whilst fighting
Our own resistance against this disease.
And so we cry out from the canopies:

No winter shall abate this spring's increase.

Disperse
Hannah Ludlow

Disperse.
Disband.
Disunite.

Police forced to separate loved ones
Through the day and through the night.

Groups of friends,

lovers,

families,

Torn apart by this Covid storm,
Told to disperse,
disband,
disunite,
By these foes in uniform.

What a tragedy it is
To be told 'please go home',
Oh what a tragedy it is
To have your social life postponed.

But when the real tragedies are displayed,
In death tolls, stories and loss,
Can you consider how your sacrifice
Is worth this considerable cost?

So whilst you sit safely at home,
And work, and dream and mope,
Don't question the intent of these forces,
Who are finding it hard to cope.

The police are human like you,
They don't want to spoil the fun,
But their job is to disperse the public
So that one day this virus is done.

Feds, pigs, the filth
Are just some of their descriptors,
But you wouldn't be using these words
If you were no longer the victors.

Necessary evil is the basis of lockdown
Giving us months of sorrow,
But if we turn the tide and respect our police,
We will see a brighter tomorrow.

Dedicated to my mum and all the other police officers working around the clock to protect the public by enforcing Covid-19 safety regulations.

Masks and Gowns
Ralph McTell

When we're at war a soldier's gun
Protects him from what might be done
By an unseen enemy waiting to take him down
But look at the workers in the NHS
Marigold hands and bin-bag vests
No PPE and not enough masks and gowns.

Promising there's enough supplies
Denies what we see with our own eyes
Truth would be a breath of sweet fresh air
Hold up your hands, admit mistakes
Denial adds to each heartbreak
Loved ones fighting for their very lives out there.

Bang on your drum do what you can
Stand at the door and clap your hands
It's the way to say we think you are the best
Stick to the rules, support the cause
Keep your distance, stay indoors
And thank your lucky stars we've got the NHS.

Statues of heroes in every town
Time we had one in a mask and gown
Stood with Nelson in Trafalgar Square
Each Carer, Doctor, Nurse who's died
Carve their names with grateful Pride
Their sacrifice almost too much to bear.

What carers earn fills me with rage
Risking their lives for the minimum wage
Holding the frontline with no barricades
All for the want of a gown or mask
Surely it's not too much to ask
The bravest carry on though still afraid.

Bang on your drum do what you can
Stand at the door and clap your hands
It's the way to say we think you are the best
Stick to the rules, support the cause
Keep your distance, stay indoors
And thank your lucky stars we've got the NHS.

More on the background to the poem and image and the associated petition,
can be found in Ralph and Ron's respective biographies, pages 216/218.

Illustration © Ron Kiddier

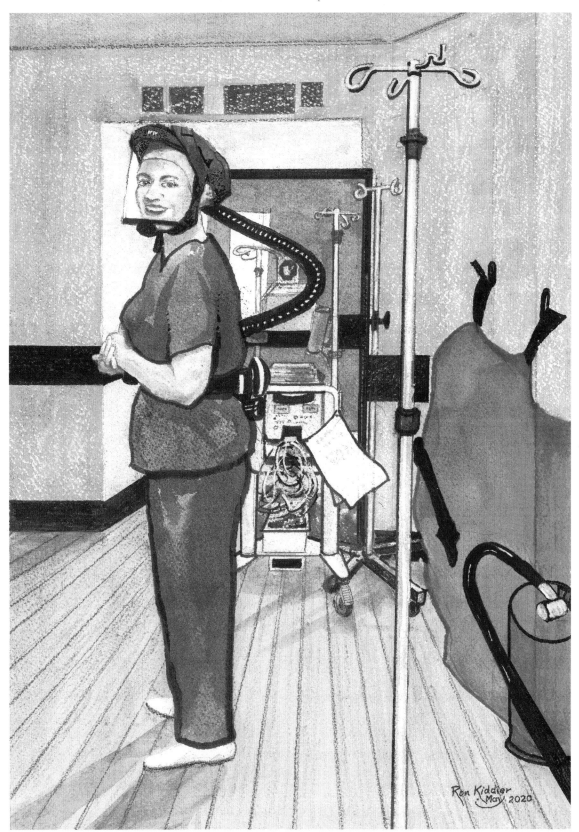

Illustration © Marisha Bewley

Heligan
Bev Bewley

Green glinting glade
There a mossy maiden sleeps,
She takes my breath away;
Her lichened cheeks, her ivied curves,
Her stroke softs the earth,
Mother and child.

A single
butterfly
lands on her lips,
A whisper of wings only she can hear,
And with the faintest flicker, she flies,
A silhouette against a cauldroned sun.

Shadows ink in as the light sobs away,
The first bat slaps the sky,
Leathern winged, brewing powerful trouble.
The owl's shriek shears through the trees,
Snags on their mesh, screaming for her sisters;
They are gathering.

Why when the wind cracked her cheeks and
Spitting fires, spouting rain were her reluctant resort,
Did too few listen to her warning words?
Who can blame her now
If she bows her head to take her crown,
To punish ingrateful man, to protect her own?

The culling comes.
Unreal shudders real.
Unsighted before an eyeless enemy within.
But in the black suck of fear, we
Grasp a hand, hand after hand offered now,
Growing a love which restores her faith,

Sending the sun to soothe,
Birdsong to balm, not blame,
The salve of a joyous, juicing earth,
For her once undeserving children,
Who when strong again, will continue the
Healing of Heligan.

*(Inspired by the Mud Maid at the
Lost Gardens of Heligan, Cornwall
and with a nod to King Lear)*

195

Rings
Bev Bewley

Alpha. A black hole.
A corona shone
Around a long lost world,
Nesting
in a nebula of dust.

Hooked down from its dark roost,
Wings flap, fluff flurries,
Flecking the mirror
where I catch
A reflection – reddened eyes, dark circles.

Pink blocks prod from every page,
Holdings words of once such import,
I chanted them, posted them on every surface,
Notes blooming like neon blossom
Only to flutter down and bright blush the floor.

Maupassant, Voltaire, Beauvoir, Zola,
Grillparzer, Goethe, Storm, Boll,
Virgil, Cicero, Ovid,
Silhouettes like continents
Imploring to be explored.

A torch globes
Round the burrows of my mind, and lights on
A craving for those cavernous libraries
Echoing with books, the hive of hungry learners
The humming honey lights as we worked till late.

I chose to soar out,
Only to swoop down low, tempted by the fruits of love, family, vocation,
No regrets, they tasted so sweet, but am I hissing excuses?
Now I'm thirsting, the cup's just out of
Reach.

Silted memories
Buried under 'wash at 30°, work at 8, shop at 3,
The eternal question what's for tea?
Cuffed by chores, the everyday,
I do for them, don't think for me.

Soon I could be spouting hoops, like a circus freak,
How I pray those pronged purple planets won't snatch my last shot,
Words wheel overhead, *Verba volant, scripta manent.**
Got to live the dash till the lid closes and I
Float out to Omega.

I started to write Rings before lockdown, after spotting a dusty ringbinder containing my university literature essays on a shelf and hankering after those days again. I originally used "corona" in its astronomical sense to describe the shining silver ring round the black hole on the side of the ring binder, but as I continued to write the poem over the next couple of weeks the word took on a whole new significance. The crow/serpent/cup references are linked to Greek mythology and the origins of the constellations Corvus, Hydra and Crater (which incidentally are next to my own constellation, Virgo.)

* *"The spoken word flies away, the written word remains."*

Illustration © Marisha Bewley

Pandemic Low Tide in Holderness
Stephen Linstead

His hand steadies her as she descends
The salted stone, that stoutly defends
The long departed pier's crenellated gates.
Over her blonde shoulder the guardian of the fates
Of countless mariners towers tall
And spotless, secure from all
Threat of tempest and erosion
As half a mile of tarmac offers it seclusion.
Picking up a flat-faced stone
From the deserted beach, alone
Among the curving sands,
He takes his keys and in his hands
Freezes her and that scene in time
Scratching its contours as shrikes climb
And wheel
Across the grey sea; a solitary seal
Briefly breaks the wave
and is gone. They stay to brave
The cool autumnal sunset
Gazing East beside a flamed-flocked rivulet.
Is their embrace haunted by a notion
That the endless timeless sea
Might not be love's possibility
But a ravenous pragmatic ocean
That carries a threat that will surely eat
Bodies old and young as street by street
It devoured those villages lost to God:
Sand-le-mere, Waxholme, Ravenser Odd;
The names that linger on the tongue,
Monkwike, Owthorne, Dimlington;
The ones young lovers give no thought on:
Out Newton, Ravenspurn and Horton;
All worn away from terra firma,
Newsham, Northorp, Kilnsea, Turmarr;
Who three miles out upon its floor
Dissolve into its tidal streams
And washed up on this sandy shore
Return as nought but trampled dreams?

Illustration © Julie Gough

The Cytokine Storm
Ruth Roberts Owen

Tipped
from our lifeboats without
warning we are
flailing. The cold
indifferent current is carrying us
away …

The familiar
lands of work and
play, family and
friends
our ritual celebrations
and even the dignity of our grieving
are revealed as so much flotsam and
jetsam in the face of the
brutal
white-topped waves
thundering
towards us.

Illustration © Bryan Ledgard

Silent Spring
Paul Thwaites

Through curtain calls, the encore of the sky
Still being itself with daily flourishes,
Wakens morrows hope from all her sorrows,
Dark certainties of the starred eyes
Of souls who soar the sleep sparked heavens,
Whilst sad worlds weep.

Birds build in their hope and blossom blows,
Pink confettis on this silenced spring,
We wed to here, too soon divorced,
In isolate remorse and swift purloining of the breath
We ring to here in death.

Waken May's green this desert air,
Loose chained streets to sing –
Borne with palms and paeans of release,
Sweet grieving last being wakened from despair,
And mute the season's weeping undertone,
Binding hands to bid us walk alone.

This silenced Spring, sun holding truth to bring,
To burdened earth the winging encore of the sky,
And we the sea kin bound,
By these chained feet of clay,
To this bane Spring and silent Day.

Illustration: 'Guardian' © Graham Ibbeson

When I Thought You Were Gone
Paul Thwaites

When I thought you were gone,
I didn't know what to do?
Hole up in a pub, drink a pint or two –
Exchange old stories
Like we do,
Some bruised philosophy,
That time has made of you, of me.

We are the crop's cream, the 'Strange Brew',
And so I went back to the 'crazy-space',
Where all that's left's to pray
And once again I walked like some forest beast
Anticipating rain.
But yet you came back,
Even though I thought you were gone,
And God, yes, now I know
There's use in the sun.

What am I except
A striver for words
I try to grasp them
But they're away like birds.

Therefore in these speechless days
What to do but wait
Dare to dream, tempt fate.
I thought you were gone, but here
You come again, let's go
Make an encore of our show
Let's drink, discuss and remonstrate
Be great,
Happy with the winds that blow
Let's wait.

Illustration: 'Tom' © Graham Ibbeson

High Numbers
Paul Thwaites

High numbers have no meaning, but the one
That multiplies in grief its mutant strain,
Makes a wall too thick to penetrate,
With time, or reason, fathom or surmount,
Such hurried loss, glossed quickly to become,
Less painful in withdrawing from this leger life.

Is no less done than the sea mined multitudes –
A number we can scrawl upon that wall,
Roll-mustered in the maths of time,
Immured and solipsistic in our solitude
Of binary existence –
Of we who are that number,
And we who see that number,
And who are by that number numbed.

Illustration: 'High Numbers' © Graham Ibbeson

Charlottes and Garlands

A haibun for Anne McPake (Anne Genner Crawford)
Mel Ledgard

Sunniest May on record then June downpours: your beloved
garden bursting with leaf, petal and branch. You hoped you
would see summer's best but winter came early instead.
Confined to bed in your queen post room, cats curled, you held
out your hands to me.

> shielding
> the comfort of touch
> denied

Your washed-white studio with its mullioned windows; all the
implements of your art. Drawers full of disembodied doll parts –
eyes, heads and torsos, arms and legs. *Carillons à musique*. Frozen
Charlottes and Maidens' Garlands. Richness of colour, delicacy
and detail. Fragments and memories. Patterns and mendings.
Impermanence.

Imprint. Legacy. Cherished work. Generations taught who
remember and pass on the gift. The kindness in items of beauty
you made me: the exquisite appliqué bag in purples and blues;
photographs of our Moon in a handmade paper album.

> memorial garden
> the celebrant wishing
> she could hug

*We lost our friend and neighbour of 25 years in June 2020,
not to Coronavirus but to cancer.*

Illustration: 'Maiden's Garland' © Anne Genner Crawford

N H S
Paul Thwaites

Now Heaven Sent our gentle warriors come,
No clarion calls to battle, no hollow drum,
Sounding its futile roll,
That spurs them through this vale of tears,
Releasing precious breath from captive air,
Where feathered Death wings, waiting on each soul
And does not spare,
These who have fallen on his spears.

No Heart Succumbs in fear,
From duty turns,
Or risk of death.
And here true kindness burns ~
And fire of cause.
Masked love brings breath,
Hearts show no countenance,
But bear the task
And dedication is their sustenance.

New Heroes Serve, a new wind blows,
From battle's midst a different freedom grows,
Love is blind, they say, that fights such foes
Invisible, but these are bound,
Even whilst defeated dead lie round,
To forge still forward and in blindness grope,
Driven by their passion and their hope.

New Hope Survives, when marshalled by the brave,
Who mourn for loss, yet every life they save,
Swells victory and these, who may, remain,
Their fallen brothers sing with praise ~
Men making chorus of these days,
When hymned defiance is our last refrain.

Nations Hear Songs before unheard,
One Nations choir, united in one word,
Let that be Harmony, to set our people free
From fears shackles, which have bound,
Let their example spread the world around,
These gentle warriors, who soft to battle come,
And bring a message for Eternity.

Illustration: 'Down to Earth' © Graham Ibbeson

Biographies

Mark K. Allen is an artist based in Edinburgh, usually venturing around darker realms of the horror genre. He is most notably known for his work published under the *Frightfeast Comix* monicker and more recently America's infamous and legendary *Gore Shriek* series. For this book, his inking accomplishments were significantly softened by the pencil-sketching talents of his wife, Aneta Horodecka-Kwiatek.

Paul Almond was born 1981 in Coventry, a city immortalised in that year's top single, The Specials' 'Ghost Town'. Moving to Suffolk lacked variety, but craving new places and faces, studying English in Sheffield offered a welcome solution. While travelling Asia, Australia and Nepal, 2 years disappeared before he returned to Sheffield and a Social Work Masters degree and stayed.

Alan 'Archie' Andrews is a former miner who worked as a fitter at Goldthorpe from 1979–1992. After a 30-year IT career, 14 spent in the USA, Alan returned to the UK and gained a BA 1st Class Hons in Illustration and Concept Art. He now spends his time developing visual media for national and international coal mining heritage projects. His work mainly focuses on digital productions including 3D modelling, animation and virtual reality showcases.

Howard Aynhoe is a digital artist and creator of trompe-l'œil. He trained in Yorkshire as a graphic designer and interpreter of printed ephemera, and utilises many found objects in his work. A long-standing member of the Tufty Club, he is also the proud owner of a Blue Peter badge.

Lee Baskerville is a 50-something local government officer and part-time amateur poet, pedant and logophile. He thinks in rhyming couplets far too much for his own good. He is also a massive music fan of many genres and surmises that his lyric efforts emerge from his many years of listening.

Beverley Bewley (nee Whitehall) lives in Glossop with her husband Dr Richard Bewley. They have two daughters, Maya and Marisha. Inspired by Maya starting to study English Literature at the University of York and with time provided by lockdown, she returned this year to the creative writing she loved as a child.

Marisha Bewley was born in 2004 and has a love of nature, animals and drawing. During lockdown she has been able to fulfil her passion for digital art and was happy to volunteer her skills for this project.

Terry Brookes is Barnsley's first and only pop artist. The foundation of his aesthetic lies on the one hand in his northern working class heritage: Albert Hirst pork pies, Barnsley Bitter, black pudding and the famous Barnsley chop. On the other it is sustained by an acute sense of absurdity and the humorous side of everyday urban existence – which for Terry is not on the side, but front and centre. In the middle of the same is an incisive yet intuitive grasp and encyclopaedic familiarity with both popular and niche musical culture and their nuances. Terry confronts the everyday with an almost surreal series of 'what ifs' – what if The Beatles came to Barnsley? What if Elvis played the Old No 7? What if Woodstock had happened in this northern mining town? – and brings the answers hilariously and rewardingly to life. *www.BROOKESart.com*

Elizabeth Brown is an undergraduate student at the University of York, studying English. She is passionate about raising awareness of hidden disabilities from which she has suffered for most of her life – like M.E./Chronic Fatigue Syndrome.

Granville 'Danny' Clarke FRSA began a long professional career interrelating the arts with folk's Foggy Dew-O, appearing on over 500 TV and Radio programmes, notably Granada's *Scene at 6.30* and YTV's *Calendar*, and recording three albums for Decca. His first integrated arts performance was in 1977 and he is both a published poet and leading watercolour artist listed in *Who's Who in the Arts*. He served as art expert and judge on Channel 4's *Watercolour*

Challenge series. His contributions are based on his own recollections of hospitalisation in Brentwood, Essex in 1980, and Barnsley, South Yorkshire in 2018. *www.granvilledclarke.co.uk*

Jeannie Clarke has been a professional muralist and illustrator for over twenty years and has many local and international clients. Her murals have appeared on BBC television including the iconic *Auf Wiedershen Pet*. She is an accomplished equestrian artist – particularly obsessed with movement and has transferred this passion to the human figure working with National Dance Company (Wales). Currently she is very excited to be working with Rambert Playground. (Also proud daughter of poet Maurice Rutherford and illustrator of his book *Random Jottings*). *Instagram: jeannieclarkeartist* *www.jeannieclarke.com*

Heath Common has been around a bit. In his youth he visited the US and got down with the beatniks and bluesmen who played and hung in Greenwich village. Then he lingered in London when the Sixties were still swinging, soaking up the scene and singing the blues. He started a family and got a proper job and by the 80s he was a headteacher by day and touring the country by night backing the Indie chart-topping *Rhythm Sisters*. More recently, as a performance poet and speaker, he undertook a gruelling tour of women's institutes. *R2* magazine called him 'utterly inspired' and 'refreshingly original'.

Stephen Cox is originally from Manchester but now lives on high land in the Highlands. He describes himself as 'a tall tale teller, dry wit, teacher and crofter. A cartoonist who knows when to draw the line, and a Buddhist who is getting there but hasn't got a return ticket'.

Anne Genner Crawford was originally from Durham and trained in Sunderland and Birmingham. She began exhibiting professionally in 1978 with exhibitions in Sheffield, The Yorkshire Sculpture Park, The Gault Gallery and the Mansfield Arts Centre, Ohio, USA. She has exhibited with her husband John A. McPake in Sheffield, Ashton-Under-Lyne, The Dean's Cloisters

and St. George's Chapel, Windsor Castle, The Portico Gallery, Manchester and The Cooper Gallery, Barnsley. Her work is in private collections in the UK, France, Germany, Australia, USA and South Africa. Anne was awarded South Yorkshire Artist of The Year in 1986. During the production of this book, Anne sadly passed away.

Chloe D'Arcy is an MA student at the University of York. She is particularly interested in how trauma and space intersect in literature. She runs *@yorpoetica* (Instagram) publishing student poetry by fellow York students, alongside *www.honeyed paper.com* where she shares her own work.

Liz Deakin A poet and artist living on the west Wales coast, Liz published four themed books of poetry while living in Bradford. She is currently publishing a fifth, *Open Your Eyes*, which tells the story of the move from Yorkshire to Wales by herself and her husband Quentin seven years ago.

Chris the Poet Dibnah is a performance poet and compere of the UK festival and traveller community, who lives in Cardiff. He has performed widely across the country and has been published in outlets including *International Times*.

Edsard Driessen is a British-born poet and wordsmith of Dutch origins. He uses his intricate international background to form the experiences which are put on the page. He continually captures ordinary moments in life and throws them into unfamiliar situations, creating new images that cast hooks into the imagination and are unafraid to question the status quo.

David Driver is a Yorkshire writer, poet and broadcaster. He has written several short story collections, a number of poetry anthologies and a sci-fi novel aimed at younger readers. He hosts 'The Writers Bookshelf' every Tuesday for Drystone Radio, which showcases writing talent at all levels. When writing poetry, he uses the pen name Arthur G. Mustard. He also directs the Gingerlicious Company, providing people with a platform and voice via storytelling and broadcasting.

Tia Duff is an English Literature student at the University of York. She mostly enjoys reading poetry and doesn't often write but gave it a go for this publication! Tia also runs an art Instagram account @*tiaduffart*, where she shares her work.

Rosemary Evans is a London-based writer. Her poetry has previously been published in the University of York's *Looking Glass Anthology* and her recent writing for stage has been produced by Slackline Productions. She has just graduated from the University of York and is working on her first novel.

Rachel Feldberg has just finished an MA in Eighteenth Century Studies at the University of York and started her PhD in September 2020. She spent her working life in the arts, most recently as Director of Ilkley Literature Festival. She's a playwright whose work has been broadcast on BBC Radio 4 and former Artistic Director of *Red Ladder Theatre Company*.

Barry Fox took his name after seeing the message 'Happy 40th Barry Fox' plastered on a fence once. He's not really 40 and he's not really called Barry Fox. He makes art in a variety of forms including painting, sculpture and collage, sometimes using found materials, in a variety of styles that often confront each other in the same piece. His world, for it is indeed quite a unique space, is original, quirky, often surprising to the point of being shocking, and frequently hilarious. He has work displayed around the world but has shown mostly in galleries in the North East of England. *www.barryfox.co.uk*

Robin Garside is a musician, producer, arranger and painter from Sheffield. The inspiration for his work can be found in South Yorkshire and the Peak District. His paintings are mainly landscapes, seascapes and figurative work using oils, watercolour and acrylic, and drawings in pencil or ink. He also leads art and music workshops around South Yorkshire.

Helen Geddes is an art historian who trained at the Courtauld Institute of Art, London, and the University of Warwick, with a doctoral specialism in the art of the Italian Trecento. She has taught on aspects of Italian art at the Open University and the University of Cambridge.

Julie Gough has extensive teaching experience at Grimsby Institute and North Lindsey College. She has been a lecturer in Critical Studies within the BA Hons Fine and Applied Art programme, an external moderator for the Open College Network and a community artist for Artlandish Community Arts. Her work has been included in many exhibitions in Lincolnshire. *https://www.juliegoughukartist.co.uk*

Paul Gough is a musician/artist living near Cleethorpes, Lincolnshire. He studied art in Grimsby and then specialised in ceramic sculpture at North Staffordshire Polytechnic. After gaining a teaching diploma in Liverpool, he taught in Barnsley and for many years in Cleethorpes, specialising in ceramics and photography. Although concentrating on music, he occasionally produces ceramics and artwork.

Gareth Griffith spent 14 years teaching English Literature as a medievalist at the University of Bristol and is now studying in London for ordination in the Church of England.

Jed Grimes has a longstanding career as a touring musician, broadcaster, and BBC R2 Award-nominated producer and arranger of traditional music, travelling the country from his home in North Tyneside. He has held many art/music/literacy workshops in schools and colleges around the UK. In recent years, Jed has been increasingly noted for his acrylic and watercolour landscape painting, and has revived an early interest in graphic novel-style line-and-wash illustration for his work here. Jed is currently working on a couple of further illustrated books of his own, including one with links to traditional song. *www.blueguitarmedia.com www.jedgrimesmusic.co.uk*

Mike Harding is a singer, songwriter, multi-instrumentalist, comedian, author, poet, playwright, broadcaster, photographer, traveller and filmmaker. In 1975 the record 'The Rochdale Cowboy' flung him into the mainstream of live entertainment, resulting in his own regular TV series, extensive radio work, decades of concert tours and over 20 albums. The breadth of his work also extends to over 40 books and plays and his writing has ranged from comedy to church architecture, fell-walking to fly-tying, short stories and novels, with many of his books illustrated with his own photographs. He has published eight volumes of poetry, the most recent being *The Connemara Cantos, Fishing for Ghosts* and *Cosmos Mariner,* and has recently completed a new play. For 15 years the highly-regarded presenter of the Folk, Roots & Acoustic Music programme on BBC Radio 2, his warmth, good humour and relaxed erudition can now be heard on his regular podcast at *www.mikehardingfolkshow.com www.mikeharding.co.uk*

Violet Hatch was born in Buckinghamshire and moved to York in 2017 to read English literature. She has enjoyed reading and writing poetry since she was nine years old, an interest which has flourished over her time at university. Her poetry is concerned with themes such as memory, nostalgia, home and family. She intends to continue to write and study next year as she embarks on an MA course in London.

Amber Hawkins is a young poet particularly enthralled by the Romantic perception of Nature. Alongside this, Amber's writing is heavily influenced by the current social and political climate, which she criticises through observing modern society's effect on the natural world. As such, her style can be found to be an eclectic mix of new and old.

Isabel Head is a second year student of English at The University of York with a particular interest in Old English texts and Norse myth.

Tony Heald has been involved with visual arts as a teacher and illustrator all his adult life before becoming a full-time professional artist, producing paintings and drawings in a variety of media but mainly in oils. He has since exhibited his much sought-after work nationally and internationally and his published artwork has a worldwide distribution.

Ray Hearne grew up in a Yorkshire Irish family in industrial Rotherham, the noisily thumping heart of Britain's industrial empire. He studied at the University of Essex, and became involved in community education. He developed his writing and performing style nurtured by the two traditions: the blarneying, expressive, lyrical, romantic, somehow feminine Irish, and the more reticent, unornamented, grittily realistic, frequently monosyllabic, more masculine Yorkshire. Over the past 30 years Ray's songs have become South Yorkshire icons, but his poetry deserves equal attention. *http://rayhearne.co.uk*

Jane Hilberry is Professor of Creativity & Innovation at Colorado College. She has published several books of poems, most recently *Still the Animals Enter*, from Red Hen Press in Los Angeles. Hilberry's great joy is to connect people with the sources of their own creativity.

Eth Holmes is a barely matured 59-year-old still clinging to the 70s. Her family is her number one passion. She likes to think she's creative, though in no specific area, as anything with a quirky slant becomes a new avenue for her to explore, poetically or otherwise.

Dave Howarth is a Sheffield-based illustrator and cartoonist. He has been drawing commercially since 1980, specialising in character development, cartoon strips, book illustration and corporate identity. His clients include CBeebies, *The Beano*, Sheffield City Council, Sheffield Wednesday, QPR and London Wasps. Taking a sideways look at a brief is what he does best. *www.hmdesigners.com*

HTH is an MA student of Fine Art at Birmingham City University and focuses on religion through contempary mixed media.
https://hyenathehermit.wixsite.com/hthehermit

Rozana A Huq is the Founder and Director of RHM Training, UK. She is an organisational behaviourist, lecturer, author, leadership coach and philanthropist. She achieved her PhD from Queen's University Management School in Belfast, Northern Ireland. Her inspiration to write comes from her interest in the history and cultures of different countries of the world.

Graham Ibbeson has been a professional artist and sculptor since graduating from the RCA in 1978. Sometimes known as 'the people's sculptor', and recently called the World's Funniest Sculptor, his celebrity bronze sculptures can be seen in over 40 towns and cities across Britain. His statue of Eric Morecambe, in the comedian's eponymous hometown, was unveiled by the Queen. Graham has also unselfishly created several memorials to mining disasters and communities. His fine artwork has been widely collected and exhibited internationally. *www.grahamibbeson.org*

Sophie Ioakim is an artist and writer of poetry from Norwich and a student of English Literature at the University of York. Her illustrations often accompany poetry as she seeks to create multi-dimensional art by bridging the gap between the visual and the literary.

Roseanna Kettle is a first-year PhD student at the University of York in the Centre for Eighteenth-Century Studies. Her research concerns emerging local literary identities during the British Industrial Revolution and her poetic compositions seek to similarly capture the intersections between science, nature, consciousness and memory.

Ronald Kiddier was born in 1924 and has been a painter almost his whole life. He painted during active service in Italy during WW2 and continued during his civilian career as a signwriter until his retirement. He then spent several years as an art coach in an Essex hospice, an experience he describes as rewarding to both him and his students. After moving to Hampshire he started painting local villages and rediscovered his love of art. Ronald is currently visited weekly by a befriender whose daughter is a doctor in a London hospital and who was photographed in PPE during the Covid-19 pandemic. Ronald created his version of this image in recognition of the efforts of all NHS workers.

Jenny Knight retired from teaching as a Senior Lecturer at the University of Brighton, from where she obtained her PhD, during lockdown 2020. Jenny has a background of working in large public-sector organisations responsible for leadership development and also ran her own management consultancy company. She also has an alternative background of writing, directing and acting and writing, performing and publishing her own poetry.

Monika Maria Kostera is a Polish humanist and economist, professor of management and organisation theorist. She is known for her contribution to business studies, organisational archetypes and myths, storytelling and narrative analysis in organisational anthropology. She holds professorships at Jagiellonian University in Kraków, Poland and at Södertörn University in Sweden. She has had three books of poetry published, and her poems set to music by Tommy Jensen on his album *Songs to a Street Poet*.

Louise Larkinson was a lecturer at York St. John University before she retired in 2010. She writes poetry and plays and is an active member of Script Yorkshire and York Playback Theatre – a form of improvised theatre enacting people's stories within a wide range of communities through drama and music.

Brian W. Lavery spent 30 years in various senior roles in journalism before undertaking a doctorate in creative writing at the University of Hull. He now teaches creative writing and journalism at the University of Leeds. His prose includes the books *The Luckiest Thirteen* and *The Headscarf Revolutionaries*, the latter of which gave rise to the song cycle *12 Silk Handkerchiefs* written by Reg Meuross, with which Brian toured the UK.

Brian has also featured on BBC Radio 4's *Four Thought* series. Planet Publications (Wales) has published his short fiction over the years and Other Poetry, About Larkin and the Larkin Press have published his poetry. In August 2020, Brian received the City of Kingston-upon-Hull Lord Mayor's Civic Crown Award for Preserving Hull's Heritage.

John Law is now retired after a varied career as a fitter, semi-pro musician and poet. He graduated in ecology from the University of York in 1994, and is a well-known naturalist, birder, botanist and keen artist. For the last 15 years of his career he worked as a re-engagement teacher at Mexborough School.

Francesca Lea actively promotes sustainability and writes with current issues in mind. Recently, she has set up an enterprise which is sustainably driven, and through her experience in a Green Impact Audit, wants to work with nature, not against it. This is her second poem to be published.

Pamela Leadbetter was widowed relatively young but has a great life living with the best dog in the world, buffered by the love of family and friends. Plants, music, herbal medicine and photography are some of the passions bringing light to her everyday life.

Bryan Ledgard is a professional graphic designer, commercial illustrator and editorial photographer. He gained two design degrees in Manchester and became Senior Designer for Macmillan Publishing in Fleet Street and Art Director for Octopus Books, part of the Hamlyn Group, in Mayfair, London. He later formed a design agency, Ledgard Jepson Ltd, in South Yorkshire which expanded to New York, USA. He has designed numerous books and journals over four and a half decades, and his photographic and illustrative work has appeared in publications worldwide.
www.bryanledgardphotography.com

Mel Ledgard is a retired multimedia, website and graphic designer with a BA (Hons) in Silversmithing & Jewellery and an MA in Writing. Latterly working for an independent radio and TV production company as a BBC Radio 2 website content producer, she now spends her time doing this and that and occasionally trying to regain creativity.

Isabelle Lepore is an undergraduate student of English & Related Literature at the University of York with a penchant for Medieval prose. She has experience reciting published poetry and performing her own pieces at national and regional competitions, and in local spaces including the York Theatre Royal. Her poem is her way of remembering her Nonno, and Italian roots, throughout the pandemic.

Nicholas Linstead was the originator of the concept of this book. By day, he is a mild-mannered, unassuming customer service agent, which he has done for a variety of public and private sector organisations. By night, however, his alter ego Bizarre Nicholas II is something of a minor legend in niche underground music circles, having founded the original Blastonbury Festival in 2007.

Stephen Linstead is Professor of Management Humanities at the York Management School, University of York. He has degrees in English and American Literature from the Universities of Keele and Leeds, and in Management from Sheffield Hallam University. He has been a musical performer on stage, radio, TV and record and has also published and performed his poetry. He recently became an award-winning filmmaker.

Hannah Ludlow is a third year English and History student at the University of York. She spends a lot of her time writing poetry, and has found this period of lockdown to be an inspiring one, allowing her to write about numerous personal experiences.

Sophie Lutkin is a reader, writer and young scholar of literature. Serving as the 2017-2019 Young Fenland Poet Laureate, she has also written poetry inspired by her visit to Holocaust camps Auschwitz-Birkenau, and is the recent recipient of the Ruth Selina Poetry Prize.

Ian McMillan is one of the UK's best-known contemporary poets. His prodigious output includes books (for adults and children), regular journalistic columns, libretto, scripts and plays. He has also made frequent appearances on television, on all the national BBC radio channels, in diverse newspapers and magazines, and as a poet in residence in places as incongruous as Barnsley FC and the English National Opera. As this might imply, he is one of the few poets able to remain completely accessible while exploring sophisticated literary techniques – exemplified by his Radio 3 show, *The Verb*, which he dedicates to 'the magic of discovery, the excitement of living language, stories, songs, the continuum of audience and writer and reader'.
http://www.uktouring.org.uk/ian-mcmillan

Becky McMurray is an established artist and occupational therapist who has worked in both the NHS and private sector. Becky specialises in book illustration, portraiture and multimedia projects.

John A. McPake is from Merseyside. He studied at Wallasey School of Art and at Liverpool, Birmingham and Leeds Polytechnics. He is a Fellow of the Royal Society of Painter-Printmakers and has been President of Manchester Academy of Fine Arts. He has exhibited widely in the UK, including several Summer Exhibitions at the Royal Academy and various one man shows. His work has appeared in overseas exhibitions including Paris, USA, Russia and several Print Biennales in Seoul, South Korea. John's work is also in public and private collections in the UK, France, USA, Germany, Norway, Australia, South Africa and Russia.

Stephanie McRobert lives in Market Bosworth in the Midlands with her wonderful family. She discovered a love of painting during retirement and art has filled her days. She recently published a book for children, set in the countryside around her home, that she wrote and illustrated.

Ralph McTell is arguably the UK's most sustainedly successful singer-songwriter in the folk idiom. Already established in the late 60s, his songwriting won him an Ivor Novello award in 1975 for *Streets of London* and more recently he was the recipient of lifetime achievement awards from the BBC Radio 2 Folk Awards and the UK Parliament All Party Group for Folk Music. In between lie more than 50 albums, the most recent of which, *Hill of Beans,* was voted best album of 2020 in the Folking Awards; successful TV and radio series for both adults and children; performances in some of the world's great venues like Sydney Opera House and the Albert Hall; and appearances in events as diverse as Later... with Jools Holland and the Montreux Jazz Festival. However, poetry has always been at the heart of his work – his lyrics have been published as a book in their own right, and he completed a three-year project on Dylan Thomas, *The Boy with a Note*, in 1992. He is also an activist, with his song *Bentley and Craig* being an important part of the campaign to gain a posthumous pardon for unfairly-executed Derek Bentley. His lyric for this book is part of his campaign to have the fourth plinth in Trafalgar Square occupied by a memorial to the heroes of our Health Service. Find out more, hear Ralph sing it, get the chords and sign the petition at *www.ralphmctell.co.uk*

Alice Manning is an English and History Student at the University of York with a penchant for semi-solipsistic verse and reflective sonnets. As an aspiring journalist she enjoys writing for the student newspaper. In her free time, she enjoys song-writing, bird-watching and all kinds of baking.

Ian Meade A graphic designer most of his life, but now mostly doing a bit of colouring in without the aid of a safety net. Lover of all things visual together with a wanderlust that usually involves food and wine. Long time runner, slowly and a bit reluctantly turning into a walker, a father and a grandfather. *https://ianmeadedesign.co.uk*

Lynda Rose Morgan likes to write, and perform, poetry about the everyday and small details of life. She admires writers such as Sharon Olds and her ex-tutor Julia Copus. She works with children with special needs, which has informed her recent work, and in 2017 published *Dad's Hands,* a collection of exquisite poems exploring bereavement in many of its aspects.

Sophie Norton is an English Literature student with a passion for poetry. She's inspired by the poetic works of James Tate and Caroline Bird, and is currently working on her first poetry collection. She loves mixed media collages, experimental music, and making crazy clothes to counteract fast fashion.

Ruth Roberts Owen teaches Welsh to adults and writes poetry in both Welsh and English. She writes primarily for herself as a way of helping to sort things out and has done so since she was seven years old. She enjoys performing her poetry live as it is the sound that's important for her. Please read her poem out loud with as much drama as possible!

Jenni Pascoe is a writer and performance poet with a penchant for purple, currently based in Gateshead, Tyne & Wear. She loves to play with words and rhythms, and her poetry covers topics ranging from the Crimean War to disenfranchised moths! She created and hosts 'JibbaJabba' a monthly spoken word extravaganza in Newcastle-upon-Tyne. Jenni regularly appears at events throughout the North-East of England and beyond. She won both Hexham Book Festival Poetry Slam and the Lamplight Poetry Slam in 2010.

Laura Potts has always written: academically and about her doctoral and post-doctoral research, as well as poetry and life writing. She has been a teacher in a wide range of contexts and of a wide range of subjects: in adult and community education; at York St John University and at Hull York Medical School; running schools' gardening projects; and as an Iyengar yoga teacher. She has been involved in health and environmental politics locally, nationally and internationally; and

currently looks after a number of orchards in the city and tends her own allotment.

Aidan Quigley is a poet from Shrewsbury, Shropshire. He is currently an undergraduate student, going into his third year of studying English and Related Literature at the University of York. He is also a songwriter and playwright, writing shows for the University of York's DramaSoc.

Adekunle Ridwan is a student, a poet and a writer who is very active on the Web and social media creating spaces for poets to share their work and interact. He is also a certified ghostwriter. A native Nigerian, he lives in Lagos.

Carina Riley was born in Ripon, but settled in York and had a long career in primary education. Now retired, with her husband Steve she enjoys seeing their six children and currently eight grandchildren. She comes from a very creative family and her skills find expression through many art forms.

Maurice Rutherford was born in Hull, East Yorkshire in 1922. After five years of military service he spent his adult life as a technical writer in the engineering and ship-repairing industry in Hull and later in Immingham, Lincolnshire. He discovered his talent for poetry in his mid-fifties and has since received substantial critical acclaim. He has published five poetry collections, notably with Peterloo Poets and Shoestring Press. He now lives in Westgate-on-Sea, Kent and is working on projects combining photography and haiku.

Sophie Ryall is a nineteen-year old student from South London. She is particularly involved in racial equality and change, and draws on politics to lyricize contemporary issues. Previous work includes writings about Palestinian occupation and the Migrant and Refugee experience in regional and national competitions such as Foyle Young Poets. As a young person growing up in an unprecedented time, she wanted to capture the concerns felt by many POC and their allies, reflecting the fear and frustration of seeing institutionalized discrimination magnified by

Covid. Her inspirations include Kate Tempest, Dave (the rapper) and Langston Hughes.

Natalie Saturnia is a current student at the University of York working on finishing her MA in Eighteenth-Century Studies, after completing her BA in English Literature from Cardiff University last year. Her interests include women's literary history, and in her free time she reads and reviews books, and runs a book club. Earlier this year, she helped put together a poetry collaboration raising money for OCD Action, and she enjoys seeing the ways in which literature brings people together.

Frances Sladen is an exhibited artist, currently living in York, who loves places: ancient buildings, daring architecture and wide open spaces, particularly the mountains. Using a 2B pencil she likes to capture unusual angles which might not normally be appreciated when passing by. With her husband, Josh Burnell, she is also a rising star on the national folk scene.

Joe Solo is an award-winning musician, writer, poet, activist, broadcaster and washing machine engineer from Scarborough. Acclaimed for both the passion of his performances (which include Glastonbury) and the craft of his songwriting, with 17 albums to his credit, he has also received multiple awards for his charitable activism, including 'Human Being of the Year' from the *Morning Star*. *R2* magazine called him 'the perfect protest singer'. *https://joesolomusic.com*

Cyang Stifano was born in 1995 in Caracas, Venezuela. She studied philosophy for a couple of years at the Central University of Venezuela. Those studies were interrupted as she became part of a movement against the government, and her family got very scared for her life. She left the country for a new life in London with her father and works in hospitality full-time. London has reminded her how much she likes writing.

Jessie Summerhayes is a spoken word artist and wordsmith with an obsession with words and stories. Never far from a book, a compulsive writer – poetry pours out when the mood strikes, halfway through a lecture, when cooking or in the middle of the night.

Anna Thornton graduated in English Literature from the University of York and is now completing a masters degree in Medieval Literatures and Languages at York's Centre for Medieval Studies. This is her first published poem.

Paul Thwaites is a retired teacher of special needs, and ex-miner and psychiatric nurse, living and working in West Yorkshire. He has written three collections of work, *Norse Gods, Box of Ochre,* and *Water Dancing with the Moon,* and numerous individual poems. He is interested in mythology, writing, history and the garden.

Nes Vanreil-Edwards is a born and bred Londoner who finds solace in all things deep, dark and macabre. She spent her youth playing video games and practising wrestling moves with her big brothers, then when she grew out of wrestling, went on to manage boardgames cafés around the country and set up her own jewellery shop as a side hobby. She has a BA in Music and Business from the University of East London and is also a talented mixologist.

Matthew Walker is a writer of poetry and prose from Middlesbrough, England, and is a student of English Literature at the University of York. His work seeks to merge the formal approaches of Romanticism and Modernism in order to explore, amongst other subjects, the subterranean and the archetypal.

Wallpaperflare is an online community of artists and photographers providing copyright free images for editorial illustration.

Ellen Waters is a Manchester-born student studying English at York. She was a winner of the Anna C. Price Poetry Prize and has been published by *The JFA Human Rights Journal*, *Write the World Literary Journal* and *SINK Magazine: Ramble*. She enjoys reading and drama, and plays the violin.

David Weir is Professor of Intercultural Management at York Business School, Professor Emeritus of Northumbria University, Partner at Fourth Paradigm Consulting and Professor at the University of Huddersfield. His poem 'Journeyman' was a winner in the Shetland Libraries International Poetry competition and for several years he was Poet in Residence at *The Edinburgh* pub, Wavertree, Liverpool.

Charley Wright is a Northern mum, teacher and wife with a BA in Fine Art from York St John University. She finds people the most interesting thing to draw and tries to recreate the continuous movement and moods that people express. Connections people forge are important and interesting to her, from a man to a woman or a child and a beloved toy. Her 5-year-old daughter's conversations mainly start with, 'Mummy, have you seen bunny? I love her you know!'.

Contributors' Index

KEY: **Poems**

Illustrations

Mark K. Allen — 19, 95, 105

Paul Almond — 142

Alan Andrews — 128, 131

Howard Aynhoe — 83, 132

Lee Baskerville — **65, 66**

Bev Bewley — **195, 196**

Marisha Bewley — 194, 197

Terry Brookes — 162, 181

Elizabeth Brown — **189**

Granville D Clarke — **118**, 119, **121**

Jeannie Clarke — 97, 98

Heath Common — **160, 163**

Stephen Cox — 86, 113

Anne Genner Crawford — 106, 124, 208

Chloe D'Arcy — **87, 88**

Liz Deakin — **92**, 94

Chris The Poet Dibnah — **30, 31, 32, 34**

Edsard Driessen — **134**

David Driver — **115, 116, 117**

Tia Duff — **51**, 51

Rosemary Evans — **157**

Rachel Feldberg — **137**

Barry Fox — 102

Robin Garside — 48

Helen Geddes — 35, 43

Julie Gough — 199

Paul Gough — 84

Gareth Griffith — **180**

Jed Grimes — 22, 25, 26, 91

Mike Harding — **21, 24, 27**

Violet Hatch — **184, 186, 187**

Amber Hawkins — **127**

Isabel Head — **44, 45**

Tony Heald — 29, 152, 155

Ray Hearne — **49, 50**

Jane Hilberry — **64**

Eth Holmes — **107, 108**

Aneta Horodecka-Kwiatek — 19, 95, 105

Dave Howarth — 81

HTH — 44, 45

Rozana Huq — **169, 170**

Graham Ibbeson — 16, 197, 203, 204, 210